STRIVING IN COMMON

STRIVING IN COMMON

A REGIONAL EQUITY FRAMEWORK FOR URBAN SCHOOLS

JENNIFER JELLISON HOLME
KARA S. FINNIGAN

HARVARD EDUCATION PRESS
CAMBRIDGE, MASSACHUSETTS

Paperback ISBN 978-1-68253-252-2
Library Edition ISBN 978-1-68253-253-9

Library of Congress Cataloging-in-Publication Data

Names: Holme, Jennifer Jellison, author. | Finnigan, Kara S., author.
Title: Striving in common : a regional equity framework for urban schools / Jennifer Jellison Holme and Kara S. Finnigan.
Other titles: Education politics and policy series.
Description: Cambridge, Massachusetts : Harvard Education Press, 2018. | Series: Education politics and policy series
Identifiers: LCCN 2018023078| ISBN 9781682532522 (pbk.) | ISBN 9781682532539 (library edition)
Subjects: LCSH: Education and state—United States. | Educational equalization—United States. | Discrimination in education—United States. | Urban schools—United States. | Racism in education—United States. | Minorities—Education—United States.
Classification: LCC LC212.2 .H65 2018 | DDC 379.2/6—dc23 LC record available at https://lccn.loc.gov/2018023078

Published by Harvard Education Press,
an imprint of the Harvard Education Publishing Group

Harvard Education Press
8 Story Street
Cambridge, MA 02138

Cover Design: Wilcox Design
Cover Image: US Census Bureau

The typefaces used in this book are Minion Pro and ITC Stone Sans.

To Katie, Anna, and Troy —J.J.H.

To my sister Cindy, who inspired in me a passion for justice and commitment to equity —K.S.F.

And to the parents, students, educators, community activists, civil rights attorneys, and other supporters of the interdistrict integration programs that are detailed in this book, who battled strong headwinds in their fight for social justice. We hope that our book will build upon your momentum and bridge your work with policy efforts outside of education to create better opportunities for all children.

CONTENTS

ONE

A New Lens on
Educational Inequality

NORMANDY IS an inner-ring suburban school district in the St. Louis, Missouri metropolitan area, which is one of the most segregated and unequal metropolitan areas in the country.[1] Normandy's student body is 97 percent African American and 91 percent low income.[2] It is one of the lowest performing districts in the state of Missouri, having only "provisional accreditation" status for over a decade. This status has meant that the district not only faces the challenges that come along with high levels of poverty in its student population, but it has also faced extra monitoring from the state.

Normandy gained national attention several years ago as the school district that Michael Brown graduated from shortly before his death at the hands of a police officer in nearby suburban Ferguson, Missouri, in August, 2014. The school district also featured prominently in the Peabody Award–winning 2015 radio episode of *This American Life*, reported by

Nikole Hannah-Jones and titled "The Problem We All Live With,"[3] which chronicled the story of the district's troubles.

While the Normandy district had struggled academically for more than a decade, it had been slowly making improvements until 2010, when it was forced by the state to absorb the 100 percent black and predominantly low income Wellston school district, which the state had dissolved due to low performance.[4] Wellston had been the only all-black district in the state of Missouri at the time.[5]

After the forcible annexation of Wellston, achievement in Normandy subsequently declined and, in 2012, the state completely stripped Normandy of its accreditation, triggering a provision that was put into state law in 1993 that allows students in unaccredited districts to transfer to nearby districts. This meant that students in Normandy had the right to leave and attend any school district that the Normandy district selected. Normandy selected the affluent and mostly white Francis Howell district that was thirty miles away (some say in hopes of discouraging transfers); in spite of this distance, thousands of Normandy students took advantage of the transfer option, which had the unintended effect of increasing integration in some of the area's predominantly white suburban districts. This was in many ways an ironic outcome in light of declining state and suburban support for the area's long-standing metro-wide school integration program, run by the Voluntary Interdistrict Choice Corporation (VICC), that had permitted students for years to transfer from St. Louis to mostly white suburban school systems.

The unaccreditation transfer policy was intended to be a punishment for districts that performed poorly, reducing their enrollment and ultimately their financial sustainability, under the assumption that such losses—or the threat of such losses—would spur improvement. Further, because in the eyes of the state Normandy was to blame for losing its accreditation, it had to pay for the cost of student transfers. As a result, Normandy was forced to pay upwards of $20,000 per pupil to the affluent suburban districts for every student who transferred out, as well as additional transportation costs for these students. In the 2016 school year, one in four students transferred, costing the district $1.3 million per month and leading to teacher layoffs and school closures.[6]

The transfer situation quickly became a political mess for the state of Missouri. Many parents in the suburbs were not happy with the transfers because it meant an influx of students of color and less affluent students into their community.[7] At the same time, as Normandy educators were working furiously to meet the performance targets set for them by the state, the district was buckling under the cost of payments to the suburbs and quickly sliding towards bankruptcy.

In an effort to address the situation, in 2014, state lawmakers decided to dissolve the Normandy school district; they renamed it the Normandy Schools Collaborative and stipulated that it be run by a state-appointed board. The state also laid off all teachers and administrators and required those interested in returning to re-interview for their positions. The state then gave the district a status of "no accreditation." While it seems like a minor shift in terminology, the switch from unaccredited to no accreditation had a big impact on the community, as it revoked the students' rights to transfer out of Normandy. Parents sued in court, and a county judge ruled in their favor, allowing Normandy students to continue to transfer out and receive their education at suburban schools with the cost paid by the district.[8]

Normandy's story is a dramatic illustration of the academic struggles that have afflicted segregated, high poverty school districts in the United States. The difficulties faced by the Normandy district also form the foundation for the main argument of this book: that districts like Normandy are embedded in a rigged system of structural relationships that set them up for "failure." Normandy is in a disadvantaged position within what is presently a zero-sum regional competition for tax base, businesses, middle income households, and industry, a competition that perpetuates resource inequality and racial and economic segregation. This results in an unbalanced system in which affluent communities continue to reap benefits, while communities with limited resources, like Normandy, struggle to stay afloat. The end result is that students like Michael Brown live, attend school, and work within environments that are stacked against them, and then are at risk of serious physical threat when they move into more affluent, white communities. Furthermore, educators, students, and parents within those communities are blamed for low school performance, while more affluent districts nearby cordon off their boundaries and rarely explicitly acknowledge or address the . ways that they contribute to these inequities.

Our key argument in this book is that without addressing this system of relationships—particularly the competitive dynamics of the metropolitan environment in which school districts are located and the structural inequities upon which those dynamics have been built—Normandy and the low income students of color it serves will continue to struggle. Further, current educational policy approaches, like the unaccreditation transfer law in Missouri, largely take an acontextual perspective by failing to account for the diverse local conditions in which school districts operate vis-à-vis the broader structures of opportunity in the metropolitan economy. The punitive systems of accountability and market-based reforms that have been so prevalent in the last decades, in essence, blame school districts for their struggles, and in doing so, do little to address the underlying causes of poor performance. We argue that reforming failing urban districts like Normandy requires broader, bolder policy approaches that change the underlying framework and system of relationships in which school districts are operating.

THE PROBLEM: NORMANDY AND REGIONAL INEQUALITY

As we will demonstrate in this book, the problems facing low performing and high poverty school districts like Normandy can be traced to policies adopted by many states, beginning in the early twentieth century, that allowed the new, predominantly white suburbs popping up around urban core cities to incorporate themselves into separate and autonomous municipalities. These movements were often tied directly to racial segregation, and they were the result of the advocacy of white suburbanites to have local control and isolate themselves from the nearby central cities.[9] These multiple governments then created a system of competition between local municipalities for residents, businesses, and tax bases.[10] In this system, the more affluent municipalities have, over time, been able to use their state-granted powers to exclude low income housing and zone in higher income housing, through regulations such as prohibitions on multifamily housing, minimum lot size ordinances, etc. This leaves lower income municipalities with little power in this regional competition: highly segregated and with a low tax base, they have been forced to impose high tax rates to provide basic services, leaving them unable to lure businesses or middle income residents.

Nowhere is this more evident than in Normandy. The district encompasses twenty-four of the region's ninety municipalities, yet the communities are all very small: the district serves just 3,100 students across those twenty-four cities.[11] In the early twentieth century, the municipalities making up the school district were white working- to middle-class suburbs, and the student population itself was virtually all white.[12] By the late twentieth century, however, some of the communities in the Normandy district transitioned to predominantly black after low income housing was demolished in nearby neighborhoods for "urban renewal" projects and to make room for local expressways.[13] Realtor steering and blockbusting also played a part in the racial transition in many of these communities,[14] which were then subjected to further lending and insurance discrimination. Each of these factors together fueled white flight out of the area to newer suburbs.[15]

At the same time, new affordable housing that was built in the region was disproportionately constructed in low income communities like Normandy, exacerbating existing patterns of segregation and racial isolation. Patterns like these can be seen throughout the United States.

Today, as illustrated in figures 1.1 and 1.2, the Normandy school district serves primarily low income students of color.[16] And, according to

FIGURE 1.1

St. Louis Metro: Percent Black and Latinx residents in school districts by census tract

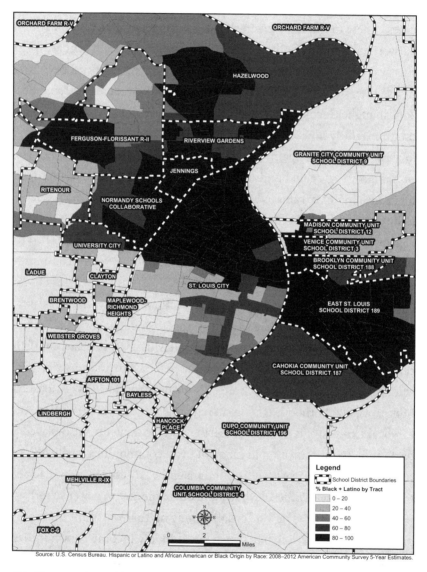

Source: U.S. Census Bureau. Hispanic or Latino and African American or Black Origin by Race: 2008–2012 American Community Survey 5-Year Estimates.

Note: The census data racial categories for this analysis were "Black or African American" and "Hispanic or Latino." Throughout we shorten those to "Black" and "Latino," respectively.

FIGURE 1.2

St. Louis Metro: Percent of individuals under 18 years old in poverty in school districts by census tract

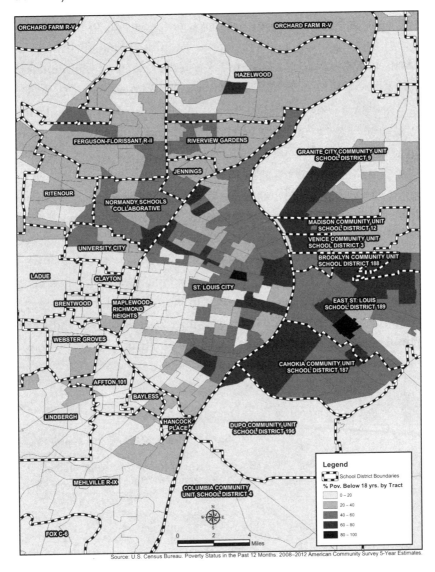

Source: U.S. Census Bureau. Poverty Status in the Past 12 Months: 2008–2012 American Community Survey 5-Year Estimates.

American Community Survey data from the US Census, the per capita income of the residents in the Normandy district is extremely low, at $17,516 in 2014.[17] Further, due to the flight of businesses and higher income residents out of the area, Normandy has one of the lowest tax bases among the districts in the St. Louis region. As a result, Normandy has had to tax itself at a very high rate—nearly double the tax rate of nearby affluent districts[18]—yet this rate yields relatively little local revenue (see table 1).

The high tax rate means that the community has a difficult time luring new businesses and non-poor residents, who have little incentive to locate in a community where they will be taxed at a high rate for very low level of services.[19] To compensate for its low tax base, Normandy increased its court fees 407 percent between 2008 and 2013, an increase of revenue from $341,000 to $1.7 million dollars. This regressive system resulted in not only an increased burden on residents, given the low income levels and high poverty rates, but it also resulted in greater conflict between members of the community and law enforcement who were increasing the number of tickets and traffic stops to shore up local revenue.[20]

In this fragmented system of government, more affluent and white families make calculated decisions to choose high income and predomi-

TABLE 1

St. Louis metro area school district tax rates and demographics

District	% white	% eligible for free/ reduced lunch 2016	2016 *school* tax rate—residential (per $100 of assessed value)	**2016 *total* tax rate—residential** (per $100 of assessed value)
Ladue	59.5%	11.7%	3.9195	7.9320
Clayton	63.6%	13.8%	3.8420	7.4528
Parkway	62.7%	19.8%	4.2163	6.9538
Ferguson-Florissant	11.1%	100.0%	5.5400	8.2775
Normandy	0.0%	91.6%	6.4292	12.3867

Sources: Missouri Department of Education and St. Louis County, 2016

nantly white school systems, those with high tax bases and low tax rates (such as Clayton, Parkway, or Ladue, in table 1) and few social needs to provide for. By choosing affluent districts, therefore, families effectively wall themselves off into their own communities, hoarding resources, opportunity, and political power.[21]

This is what we mean when we say that the system is rigged against Normandy and districts like it. Because of this unbalanced system of relationships, no matter how brilliant or creative or committed the superintendent and other educators within districts like Normandy are, they cannot overcome these underlying structural and racial dynamics.[22] This is true even *if* extra resources were provided each year to lower income schools, although in Missouri poor districts receive 17 percent less funding than affluent ones.[23] The district is then further punished by educational policy approaches like the state's accountability law, which contributes to the district's woes rather than shoring it up.

In fact, educational policy has largely focused on technical reforms within the educational system—including governance, teacher training, choice, and standards—with limited results. While school finance equity would certainly be an important step forward in terms of addressing the differential needs of schools across segregated communities, it does not sufficiently reverse the decades of discriminatory policies and practices that have impacted other aspects of students' (and their families') lives in terms of housing, community services, health care, transit, job opportunities, etc. Without a better understanding of the broader housing, tax, and economic dynamics that we just described, educational policy continues to spin its wheels in trying to improve "failing" schools.

THE FOCUS: REWRITING THE RULES OF THE REGIONAL GAME

For districts like Normandy to break out of this cycle, the structures of segregation must be tackled, along with the underlying competitive relationships (between school districts, between cities, and between schools) that drive these patterns. Headlines often focus on the symptoms of this crisis in urban areas—the concentration of poverty, cities struggling to reinvent themselves, violence—but what has not received sufficient attention are the historical trends and interconnected social and economic policies that have led us to this point in time. As Myron Orfield writes: "Central cities function within structural systems that operate across entire metropolitan areas, their housing and job markets, their transportation networks. Those structural systems must be altered before the spatial distribution of jobs, housing, and residents will shift."[24]

In this book we argue that educational policy must take a regional equity approach to tackle these issues. A regional policy approach that is focused on equity seeks to address the problems of inequality that we have described (poverty concentration, housing segregation, unequal school funding, and access to jobs and transit) by focusing on the low income communities that are negatively impacted by regional inequity while at the same time working to change the dynamics of the region as a whole.

As a 2006 report by the Conversation on Regional Equity concluded, regional equity involves broadening the lens to focus on entire regions and all aspects of children's lives:

> Achieving regional equity means considering both people and place. A competitive and inclusive region is one in which members of all racial, ethnic, and income groups have opportunities to live and work in all parts of the region, have access to living wage jobs, and are included in the mainstream of regional life. It is also one in which all neighborhoods are supported to be vibrant places with choices for affordable housing, good schools, access to open space, decent transit that connects people to jobs, and healthy and sustainable environments.[25]

Regional equity thus broadens the lens from cities to entire regions, and calls attention to the way in which competitive dynamics between cities and suburbs contribute to what continues to be constructed as "urban" problems. As Fordham political science professor Paul Kantor argues, "it is no longer fruitful to treat cities and other urban places as special interests with special problems to successfully address urban inequalities. The most critical forces now shaping urban America overwhelmingly are found beyond it."[26]

Regional equity approaches vary in structure and scope: at their most limited, they entail coordination between cities and suburbs on specific regional problems; at their most powerful, they consist of a regional governing body with policymaking powers over transit, taxation, land use, and housing.

While regional equity has gained traction in scholarly and policy debates in urban studies, education has been largely left out of these conversations to date. Although education is a key part of the diagnosis of the problem, advocates for regional equity have focused on municipal governance reforms, transit, and the environment; schools have not been a large part of the solutions that have been set forth within these conversations. At the same time, within education policy and scholarly conversations, the focus has frequently been on reforms within education alone.[27]

There is something missing, therefore, from *both* the regional equity and educational reform conversations. The education policy debates overlook the problem of regional inequality as a cause of poor educational performance.[28] The urban affairs narrative, on the other hand, largely overlooks the role of education policy as a tool (individually or in combination with these other policy tools) to address such trends. This book argues for the need for a bridge between these two largely disparate, yet interconnected, conversations.

In *Striving in Common*, we push the education policy world to consider how problems of school failure are linked to larger inequities across regions—not only in terms of segregation and inequities in school funding, but in the underlying conditions and structures that limit economic growth and maintain patterns of segregation. We also show how educational policies (particularly school choice and accountability policies) can worsen these inequalities if the underlying disparities are not taken into account.

Our book crosses disciplinary boundaries, urging regional equity advocates to engage with educational policy scholars in deliberate and comprehensive ways and to understand how including education in regional equity initiatives can bolster efforts to promote equity, thus, for example, shoring up economic development and improving housing integration through targeted supports or investments in schools in the most challenging neighborhoods. This book, therefore, is a bridge between these two disparate, yet interconnected, conversations in education policy and in urban affairs.

The book's title captures our main argument. The phrase derives from *competere*, the Late Latin root of *compete*, which means "to strive in common" (or, in classical Latin, "to come together, agree, to be qualified"). Our title is thus a play on the word *competition*—and it encapsulates our argument about the need to flip the educational system's current competitive structure towards more collaborative, regional, and cross-sector arrangements. Central to the book is the idea that growing spatial inequality has fomented political polarization that has thwarted regional equity in education and other areas that are closely linked, such as housing, economic development, and public health. This mostly comes from inaction in these areas—in fact, as political science professors Marion Orr of Brown University and Valerie Johnson of DePaul University accurately point out, even "deciding not to decide is a decision."[29]

Despite a growing awareness of the problems facing urban communities, there is a lack of a broader framework or clear policy approach to address the underlying regional dynamics that drive segregation, concentrated poverty, and racial isolation. Broader approaches must include multiple school districts across a region, and integrate or align educational policy with housing, transit, economic development, and health.

Our own work in this area began with a focus on urban education and equity, but has evolved over time into a regional equity focus. This is a result of our collaborative work over the last seven years through a Ford Foundation–funded study of one type of regional education policy: interdistrict school integration programs. These programs, adopted from the 1960s through the 2000s, seek to address segregation between city and suburban schools by allowing students to transfer across the boundaries of districts, both to create more integrated learning environments and to provide students with access to greater resources, academic and social opportunities, and networks. Varying in size and structure from nearly 600 students in Rochester, New York (the oldest program); to more than 6,000 in Omaha, Nebraska (the newest); to nearly 19,000 in Hartford, Connecticut (the largest); they have involved tens of thousands of students. Our book draws on our interviews with individuals involved in these programs in eight communities: St. Louis, Missouri; Hartford; Minneapolis; East Palo Alto (and the surrounding region), California; Rochester; Boston, Massachusetts; Omaha; and Milwaukee, Wisconsin. What we learned from these programs is that while they provide some important opportunities that almost no other educational policy provides—by addressing the problem of segregation across districts—they are woefully inadequate in addressing the underlying dynamics that created the segregation and inequity in the first place. From this work, we came to realize that there are severe limits to educational policy without a broader regional approach. Throughout this book, we include cases from this study as well as other selected cases that we have studied as part of this broader work.

POLITICS AND THE CHALLENGES OF MOVING FORWARD

The regional inequities that we point to in this book have, for the past several decades, received relatively little attention in the education policy world. One key reason for this lack of attention is that these arguments were largely drowned out by a counter-narrative that held that calling attention to these issues was tantamount to letting schools off the hook— and that, in fact, schools can and should be able to "do it alone." Another reason that these arguments received little traction is that they were often dismissed by skeptics who believed these issues were both unlikely to capture the public's attention and were politically not feasible.

The political problems are, indeed, formidable. This is in part *because* growing spatial inequality has fomented the political polarization that has often thwarted efforts to address these issues, with resistance coming from all sides (communities of color, suburban elites). In this work, we therefore employ a "political geography" framework to explain both the causes and consequences of urban inequality. This framework draws attention to the ways in which both public policy and private actors have created racialized spaces over time, and in particular to the ways in which city and school district and neighborhood boundary lines have inscribed racial inequality into geographic space.

Legal theorist Richard Thompson Ford points out that political dynamics are self-perpetuating, even after the explicitly racist policies of the past are long gone; they are reproduced from generation to generation, as the higher incomes, home equity, educational opportunities, and social networks of the wealthier communities provide access to opportunities that families of color in poor communities do not have access to.[30] These power dynamics and tensions set up a dichotomy of "us" versus "them," and they most often advantage the affluent.

Political geography helps to drive *localism*, which is another political framework we employ in this work. Localism refers to the inclination on the part of communities to promote their own interests, through either legal or political channels. Localism is thus an important political issue, especially as it is considered from the perspective of white, suburban populations as compared with the perspective of communities of color within cities or inner-ring suburbs. On the one hand, localism helps us to understand what is sometimes referred to as "opportunity hoarding" of elite suburban actors within a metropolitan system, as they consciously or unconsciously support policies and practices that benefit their own children.[31] However, localism is also associated with community control, which is one of the reasons why communities of color are sometimes lukewarm on regionalism themselves: after decades of marginalization they do not want to give up their political voice. Movements supporting community control of schools—including community schools that may remain segregated—have strong roots in communities of color, and many of these communities fought difficult political battles to gain more power and authority over local schools and to raise appropriate levels of concern that their communities might again lose if they were to consider metro-wide equity policies.

Creating a regional table for discussion, therefore, doesn't necessarily ensure that equity will be the focus, or that the families of color living in the city will have—or seek—a voice at this table and benefit from the approaches put forward. Localism therefore is critical to understanding two different perspectives: those of white suburbanites and those of leaders of color within cities as they consider approaches to ensure regional equity.

Two theories can help set a course around these thorny political dynamics and help us to think about ways to move forward: *urban regimes* and *civic capacity*. These theories, taken together, help illuminate how the capacity of a community to change lies in the ability of key actors to develop a shared focus on community problems and in the existence of a broad-based network of both elites and ordinary citizens involved in deliberation and action.

Urban regimes focus on *who* is making reforms in a city, so as to understand which reforms are pursued, which are successful, and why those are successful.[32] While the theory came to prominence with Clarence Stone's study of Atlanta in 1989, it has been used to understand how various interests are incorporated into coalitions not just at the city level but also at the regional, subcity, and neighborhood levels.[33] Rather than focusing on formal governmental actors, urban regime theory focuses on the coalitions built among governmental actors and others including business elites, community leaders, advocacy groups, citizens, etc. Just as one might consider the importance of building broad social and political coalitions across sectors within an urban community in pursuit of a common goal, so too must efforts toward regional equity consider these same strategies. Urban regimes are important to understand because they help to explain how and why metropolitan areas have worked toward regional reforms, developing a common vision around equity, in some instances and not others.

While urban regime theory is primarily focused on collaboration among actors and the resources they mobilize, at the root of any urban regime is the idea of power. Research suggests that it is important to examine not just the power elite but also the larger connections across individuals and agencies, the relationships among these members, and the resources they bring to bear on social problems, as this is what builds "civic capacity" in a community.[34] Stone and his colleagues define civic capacity as the ability of communities to interject new ways of thinking to address problems and to bring together diverse interests from a broad segment of the community in order to solve problems collectively.[35]

Linking back to our discussion of political geography above, these theories help us to understand how a community might alter the power structures aligned with these racialized spaces and develop collective efforts toward regional equity. In essence, the ability to engage a community's civic capacity relies on a variety of institutions and individuals who contribute to a shared vision, participate in the change process, and plan to maintain the community over time.[36] A closer look at the coalitions that do or do not exist in a metro area can help to explain what may be getting in the way of regional equity within education or other areas of urban policy, such as housing, transportation, health, or economic development. Such an analysis can also illuminate, in cases where regional equity has been advanced, what the process was that led community members to pursue collective regional goals despite competing local interests.[37]

CHAPTER OVERVIEW

In this chapter we have argued that there must be a stronger bridge between educational policy and the urban policy and planning worlds to allow for more closely aligned and integrated policy responses that focus on regional equity. In the chapters that follow, we further develop this argument using particular cases from our research to help illustrate these issues.

In chapter 2, we describe how the current context of inequality between school districts in metropolitan areas in the United States arose, illustrating how decades of discriminatory policy decisions at the local and state levels created deep inequities between urban school districts and their surrounding suburbs. The damaging effects of these policies—particularly the creation of intensely segregated and racially isolated neighborhoods—have been documented in a burgeoning literature on "neighborhood effects" in the past several years.[38] In this chapter, drawing upon our study of Milwaukee, we also show how and why educational policymakers and pundits have, over time, downplayed the patterns of segregation and concentrated poverty as sources of educational problems, and have focused instead on "technical fixes" to improve the performance of racially isolated and high poverty (primarily urban) schools.

In chapter 3, we describe the interdistrict school integration programs that were the focus of our study. As we show, these policies were among the few developed explicitly to address the growing segregation and inequality between urban and suburban schools that had occurred over decades. Through our case studies of two interdistrict programs, in East Palo Alto, California, and Rochester, New York, we show how these programs resulted in gains for some students, yet we conclude ultimately that such programs were like small sandbags trying to hold back a wall of water: they were ultimately unable to counteract the powerful economic and political tides that worked against them. We also show how these programs ultimately ended up being inequitable as a result of power dynamics, particularly in terms of the suburban power that constrained both the policy design and implementation, and localism on all sides.

In chapter 4, we switch gears and turn outside the education policy world for ideas. We examine the stories of places that sought to address the underlying system of relationships that create inequalities across regions through broad-based, regional solutions—places like the Twin Cities in Minnesota and Portland, Oregon. Yet we also illustrate how these solutions have missed their potential because they have largely left education off the table.

In chapter 5, we shift our focus to begin to develop our solution—a policy framework centered around regional equity in education. We begin with the story of Omaha's multifaceted regional educational policy, which went far beyond most other interdistrict programs we studied by including both place-based approaches and mobility, tax sharing, and regional governance approaches. Building on Omaha, we lay out the core elements of what a regional approach to educational and broader social inequality might entail.

Although the politics of regional equity are discussed throughout the entire book, it is in this last chapter, chapter 6, that we focus directly on the steps that are necessary to confront political geography and localism, and to build civic capacity around regional equity. We return to the underlying political theories and discuss the ways that communities can build coalitions, interject new ways of thinking, and develop a vision that aligns education with other policies, all in the pursuit of regional equity. In this chapter we also discuss what local, state, or federal courts or policymakers must do to move beyond treating the symptoms of inequity to understanding and reversing the underlying, systemic causes of urban school failure with sustainable and politically viable approaches.

TWO

Misdiagnosing the Problem
of Educational Failure

THE MILWAUKEE PUBLIC SCHOOLS (MPS) have struggled for decades. According to state report card data released in November 2016,
the district ranked dead last in Wisconsin for graduation rates, and ninth
from the bottom in overall student performance, with more than 25
percent of the district's schools designated as "failing to meet expectations."[1] Of all the failing schools in the state of Wisconsin, MPS housed
nearly half of them.[2]

The district has been frequently characterized as dysfunctional in
discussions about reform. For example, Wisconsin state senator Alberta Darling lamented when the Milwaukee School Board refused to
allow schools to be moved into her proposed state-run district for low
performing schools: "It breaks my heart to see city and school leaders
drag their feet while there are MPS schools where not a single child can
read proficiently. They are putting a failed system ahead of kids."[3] State

representative Dale Kooyenga said that district officials did a "good job of bringing absolute chaos, dysfunction, and [a] toxic environment for trying new ideas in Milwaukee."[4]

The reports of dysfunction in Milwaukee parallel reports in other major urban cores. Indeed, problems of academic failure, financial debt, and enrollment loss are reported by news media on a regular basis in many of the nation's largest cities, including Chicago; St. Louis; Washington, DC; Newark; and Philadelphia. Such problems prompted former Education Secretary Arne Duncan to label the Detroit Public Schools a "national disgrace" and Kansas City's schools as "among the worst in the nation."[5]

This perception of dysfunction in cities like Milwaukee is not new and, in fact, was largely responsible for a voucher law in Milwaukee created decades ago to allow low income Milwaukee students to attend private schools. This program, the first public school voucher program in the nation, has grown significantly since its origin in 1990, thanks in part to Secretary of Education Besty DeVos, who was integrally involved in the expansion of vouchers in the city.[6] Today, more than 40,000 students are enrolled in schools outside of the traditional system through charter schools and the voucher program, compared with just over 75,000 enrolled in traditional public schools.[7]

This blame-the-school-system approach, however, deflects attention from the extraordinarily high levels of segregation in Milwaukee schools by race and poverty. The narrative around school reform that places the responsibility entirely on schools themselves—mostly on educators and administrators—rarely acknowledges such patterns. Rather, to the extent that issues of segregation are discussed, they are often viewed as excuses by reformers who argue that problems can be solved with tougher standards, harsher sanctions, or choice mechanisms that will disrupt the dysfunctional bureaucracy that serves those students.

To understand how to address the problems of urban school failure, we argue that it is important to understand and address the roots of one key underlying cause: school segregation. Our argument is not that something magical happens when students are integrated by race and class. Rather, as john powell has noted, segregation is not inherently about the race or class of students, it is about the isolation of historically marginalized students (in the US, predominantly low income African American and Latinx students) from opportunity.[8] By isolating the privileged from the marginalized, segregation sets in motion powerful political and economic forces that propel inequality: white and affluent families use their resources, begotten through decades of advantage in housing and social policy, to channel resources away from schools serving lower income students of color, and towards their own children—thus ensuring that schools serving low income students of color are consistently undermined through a lack of both financial and political support. As the NAACP recognized in the cases leading up to and including *Brown v. Board of Education,* it is for these political reasons that separate is very difficult to be made equal, as politics and power will almost always work against segregated schools.[9]

This framework helps to explain why the educational literature has documented many challenges associated with segregated schools. Research has found that schools serving large concentrations of low income students and students of color frequently have lower levels of resources, lower teacher quality, lower teacher expectations, and less curricular rigor.[10] Further, by concentrating high-needs students on one campus, segregation can generate much higher demands on school resources and personnel, strains that can then diminish the capacity of a school to improve.[11]

It is for these reasons that educators have difficulty reforming their way out of these problems, and this is why successful high poverty schools are often said to "beat the odds," because the deck is stacked so heavily against them. One study, for example, by Tulane University professor Doug Harris, examined the likelihood of schools of differing demographics to be rated high or low performing: he found that low poverty schools were twenty-two times more likely to be high performing than high poverty schools; and that low poverty *and* low minority schools were eighty-nine times more likely to be high performing than high poverty, high minority schools.[12]

This is also why numerous studies have shown that segregation and concentrated poverty negatively affect the achievement level of students, even after controlling for a host of school quality and student background factors.[13] Stanford professor sean reardon, in a large-scale longitudinal study of state test scores from all public districts in the United States, recently found that, controlling for a host of other factors, racial segregation in schools accounted for one-fifth of the racial achievement gap.[14] Another study, by professors Russell Rumberger and Gregory Palardy, found that students switching from a low income school to a higher income school showed achievement growth on par with two years of the most effective class-size reduction program.[15] Importantly, segregation has been shown to be harmful to long-term academic and social outcomes as well.[16]

To be sure, it is important to acknowledge the deep historical problems with the implementation of school integration policies. There are many ways in which racism has undermined the implementation of such policies, making children of color bear the brunt of social, academic, and psychological costs.[17] Research has shown that students of color in integrated schools often find themselves marginalized, tracked into lower-level courses, and disciplined at higher rates.[18] Thus, creating integrated schools does not mean that they will always be inclusive or equitable.

We argue school segregation can and should be dismantled in a way that creates equitable and inclusive learning environments, and so must the larger dynamics that drive segregation, including housing policy, transit policy, and economic development policy. Addressing these larger dynamics will aid in the creation of a more equitable educational system that both reinvests in the most challenging schools and communities and begins to break down the concentration of poverty (within cities) and concentration of power and resources (outside of cities) to reduce educational inequities across regions.

In the rest of this chapter, we explain how and why the racial isolation and poverty concentration affecting Milwaukee and other urban districts have taken root. We show how these patterns of segregation were the result of decades of collusion between the government and powerful interests that carved up metropolitan areas into a system of competing jurisdictions, a system which left urban districts highly segregated, under-resourced, and politically weak vis-à-vis the suburbs that surrounded them. As segregation grew across the country, the political capacity to address these problems began to fray. At the same time, policymakers and pundits downplayed these patterns of segregation and concentrated poverty and focused instead on technical fixes such as school-choice and accountability policies. We conclude that the blame placed on urban school systems is in large part a problem of misattribution. This blame should not be placed solely on the educational system, but rather on segregation and the policies that created it.

THE INTERSECTION OF GEOGRAPHY, POLITICS, AND SCHOOL SEGREGATION: 1900S TO 1950S

In current policy discourse, school segregation is often characterized as a problem that, while unfortunate, is the result of patterns that are no one's fault, but merely the outcome of market forces and individual preferences.[19] Yet a closer look at history reveals that these patterns can be traced, in large part, to actions taken by governments, both federal policies that intervened in housing markets, and state policies that favored suburban autonomy.[20]

Segregation was not always a problem in cities. In the north, urban neighborhoods were fairly integrated until the early twentieth century,[21] partly due to the low number of African Americans living in cities at the time, as well as relatively open race relations in the north in that era. In the south, while race relations were anything but positive, neighborhoods were in fact somewhat integrated, as the southern urban residential system was one of broad avenues with large homes for whites, with homes for African Americans on smaller streets and alleys in the vicinity.[22]

This era of relative integration in cities drew to a close in the early twentieth century, as the number of African American migrants into cities—especially in the north—began to skyrocket, lured by the enhanced opportunities created by industrialization, and (for northern migrants) a desire to escape the brutality of the blatantly racist Jim Crow system in the south.[23] As the number of migrants increased, whites sought to protect their workplaces and neighborhoods through both physical intimidation and violence; when violence became unsustainable, whites invented new policies, such as restrictive covenants, to help them exclude migrants from their neighborhoods.[24] In the south, white-dominated city councils went a step further, adopting racial zoning ordinances which limited the parts of the cities in which African Americans were permitted to live. While these ordinances were struck down by the Supreme Court in 1917,[25] some cities, such as Austin, Texas, instituted more legally creative strategies to force African Americans into certain parts of town, such as providing public services (such as schools and utilities) to African Americans only if they moved to designated parts of the city.[26]

Cities possessed a great deal of political power in this era. This power was due in part to the presence of thriving industries and robust tax bases; it was also due to cities' abilities to expand boundaries to annex territory. These annexations were accomplished frequently with the consent of suburbs themselves, which was in many states required by state law.[27] As a result of this ability to annex land, cities were able to capture the majority of the population within a metro area,[28] thereby maintaining a strong tax base as well as strong political standing.[29]

In contrast to today, urban school districts also enjoyed a great deal of political power before the 1950s, with large numbers of upper-middle-class and wealthy residents still residing within their borders, attending their school systems, and serving on their city councils and school boards.[30] As political scientist Clarence Stone observes: "Although conflict was never totally absent, these systems enjoyed substantial support. They had a solid tax base, their top officials operated under an aura of professional authority, and they possessed a diverse student body with heavy representation of the middle class."[31] Indeed, there was a great deal of faith placed in the men who ran the school systems, the administrative progressives who had gained power on the platform of professionalizing the management of (and taking the politics out of) schooling.[32] Yet these progressives held sharply different expectations for minority students: at this time, ethnic minority students were seen as largely intellectually or culturally inferior, lacking in the "aptitude or appetite for advanced learning"[33]—suited not for college or white-collar occupations, but rather for the manual blue-collar jobs that were plentiful in cities at the time.[34] Such beliefs were supported by racist ideologies of intelligence that bolstered these claims with biological explanations.[35] These racist ideologies also supported the policies of separate schools based upon race that were adopted by law (*de jure*) in all southern and most border school systems, as well as in practice (*de facto*) in many school systems in the west and north.[36]

Even those few districts that were integrated in this era would grow segregated by the latter half of the twentieth century. This was primarily because of two major policy developments (one in federal policy, one in state policy) which both promoted the growth of suburbs and created racial divisions in metropolitan areas between city and suburbs.

The first major development was the intervention of the federal government into housing policy through the creation of two important federal housing agencies: the Federal Housing Administration in 1934 and the Veterans Administration in 1944. Together, these two agencies were responsible for the massive suburbanization of white families during this time.[37] The FHA was created to shore up the depressed housing market of the 1930s, and the VA was created to address housing shortages after the war in the 1940s. These agencies supported the housing industry indirectly by insuring private banks against loss and encouraging banks to provide long-term, low-cost home purchase loans. Together, these changes in private banking made home buying affordable for many more Americans than before, thereby radically increasing both home purchases and new home construction.

These newly affordable homes and home loans, however, were available only to white families who moved to the suburbs. This is because both the FHA and VA required that banks employ racially biased neighborhood appraisal rating systems that gave higher ratings to white suburban neighborhoods, and lower ratings to diverse and older urban neighborhoods. As a result, white families secured more favorable loan terms for moving out of cities and into all-white suburbs, while families of color were largely unable to secure loans at all, excluded from buying a house in the suburbs and unable to secure a loan for a city home due to unfavorable neighborhood ratings.[38] These VA and FHA policies fueled disinvestment in urban cores and created deep and lasting racial wealth disparities, as families of color became effectively locked out of the single greatest federally subsidized wealth-building opportunity of their generation.

The second significant policy development at this time was the end of annexation by cities. As noted previously, into the early twentieth century cities had successfully annexed territory as their population grew outward—partly as a result of city boosterism and the desire for many suburbs to be annexed to receive city services. In cases where suburbs were opposed, state legislatures often overrode local opposition, reinforcing the power of the cities. By the early twentieth century, however, suburbs began to fight back against annexation, using the power granted to them by nineteenth-century state laws that gave suburban municipalities the right to incorporate into their own autonomous jurisdictions.[39] These laws were more common in the north, but eventually also affected the south.[40] Resistance to city annexation efforts began with the wealthiest suburbs—and "as the suburban trend gained momentum, state legislators became increasingly reluctant to override the wishes of suburban voters."[41] In addition, in the 1930s cities themselves were less inclined to embark on annexation campaigns as they struggled to provide public services in a Depression-ravaged economy. As a result, annexation efforts by cities largely ended.[42]

This lack of annexation by cities, along with an increasing number of separate and autonomous suburbs, meant a steady decline in the proportion of city population relative to the overall metropolitan population.[43] In the south, these dynamics were somewhat different because a number of southern cities still had annexation powers through the mid-twentieth century. These annexation efforts were often undertaken to dilute the African American vote. Houston, for example, continued to expand over this time period, from 9 square miles in 1910 to 350 square miles by the end of the 1950s.[44] As a result, in those southern cases, cities did not suffer the same decline in tax base and population as in the north.

Yet outside the south, trends of suburban incorporation would effectively constrain cities for years to come. As middle-class families fled to entirely separate suburban communities, both cities and urban school districts lost tax dollars, wealthy and influential residents, and ultimately political power.[45]

1960S–1980S: DEEPENING DIVIDES AND THE BEGINNING OF THE TECHNICAL SCHOOL REFORM ERA

The city/suburban divide expanded into a wide chasm in the 1960s through 1980s, as the proportion of low income African Americans and Latinx rose in cities, while white and middle-class flight out of cities continued.[46] Between 1960 and 1970, Chicago lost 19 percent of its white population, St. Louis lost 32 percent,[47] and Atlanta lost 20 percent.[48] Between 1950 and 1970, as a result, the proportion of the city population that was African American, particularly in major northern cities, grew significantly—rising from 14 to 22 percent in Chicago, and from 16 to 44 percent in Detroit.[49] (Data on Latinx populations are not available due to the racial classifications of Latinx as white at the time).[50]

White and middle-class flight, combined with deindustrialization and the exodus of manufacturing jobs out of cities, resulted in a steadily dropping tax base in those cities that were unable to expand or annex territory. Retail business followed middle-class residents to the suburbs: between 1967 and 1977, central city retail sales dropped dramatically: 38 percent in Boston, 36 percent in Minneapolis, and 44 percent in Cleveland.[51] Some cities that lost middle-class residents tried to address the gap in tax resources by increasing taxes on city residents, which had the unintended effect of propelling further flight of those who could afford to leave.[52]

Cities that were able to annex land fared somewhat better at this time. However, some cities' annexation efforts were stalled due to racial politics. In Richmond, Virginia, for example, both minorities in inner cities and suburbanites were opposed to annexation because it would dilute their respective political power.[53] Court-ordered busing also contributed to a halt of annexation efforts in the state, as suburbanites did not want to be pulled into a city desegregation program.

Cities that could not, or would not, annex had few tools to combat the flight of middle-class families. This flight was accelerated by riots in the mid- to late 1960s, which were triggered by anger at racial injustice, segregation, and growing inequality.[54] Between 1964 and 1971 there were more than 700 uprisings across all regions of the country.[55] The uprisings bolstered federal attention to civil rights policy, but had the unintended effect of undermining political support for civil rights policies among suburbanites.[56]

The impact on school districts from these changing demographics among cities and suburbs varied by region. In the North and Midwest, white flight meant a dramatic drop in the proportion of whites in city school systems.[57] However, in the South, where districts were more likely to be countywide, white flight to the suburbs had less of an impact on the overall demographics of the school districts, as they fled to white schools within (segregated) countywide school systems.

While southern school segregation was tackled in the 1970s, thanks in large part to the US Supreme Court rulings in *Green v. County School Board of New Kent County* (1968) and *Swann v. Charlotte-Mecklenburg Board of Education* (1971)[58] that dismantled formerly de jure segregated systems, the problem of de facto city-suburb or "between-district" segregation that was more common in the Midwest and in the North came to a head in the 1974 *Milliken v. Bradley* case involving the Detroit Public Schools.[59] In this case, the Supreme Court ruled that metropolitan or interdistrict desegregation remedies for all-minority school systems like Detroit were impermissible, unless the suburbs were found to be culpable, which was very difficult to prove. As a result, interdistrict remedies were largely off the table in metropolitan areas, meaning segregated, mostly African American and Latinx city school systems in Chicago, Philadelphia, Detroit, and elsewhere were left with virtually no recourse. This ruling was particularly devastating after the 1973 *San Antonio Independent School District v. Rodriguez* decision that ruled that school funding equity was not mandatory.[60]

These court cases dealt a destructive blow to many urban school systems, which were left in a sort of fiscal and demographic quagmire, with growing concentrations of students in need and with a shrinking tax bases from which to serve them. Politically, urban districts were also in a difficult position as they were often unable, given mounting suburban power, to obtain compensatory funding from states to assist them.[61]

However, due to the radical demographic change in city school systems like Milwaukee, African American and Latinx families did gain increased power in school district politics starting in the 1960s. Indeed, in many cities, school districts were the first agency of local government that African Americans and Latinx successfully gained control of.[62] Yet, as University of Kansas professor John Rury writes of African American control of many urban districts, this represented a "hollow victory" as often these systems had a host of problems.[63] As whites moved to the suburbs, they invested their political and economic power in making suburban systems superior; corporations in this era—often led by these same suburbanites—also became less interested in city school systems.[64]

Not coincidentally, as urban school districts were growing increasingly segregated and legal avenues to integration were closing, the goal of integration began to be increasingly questioned not just by suburbanites and courts, but by leaders of color in city school systems as they reasserted their desire for community control. It was at this time that a new narrative about school reform began to gain prominence. This narrative directly challenged the importance of integration, and instead called for the creation of high performing, high quality, segregated schools, under the control of local community leadership—importantly, leadership of color that would be more responsive to the needs of the children of color that they served.

This approach was exemplified by both the "community control" movement in the late 1960s and the "effective schools movement" in the 1970s,[65] both of which were aligned with the 1965 Elementary and Secondary Education Act (ESEA). ESEA marked the first significant infusion of federal funding into US public schools and was designed to improve outcomes for "educationally disadvantaged" students through additional resources for curricular and instructional supports for low income students.[66] In fact, ESEA largely overlooked the question of school segregation.[67] Further, the effective schools movement offered a roadmap for those who wanted to improve racially isolated urban school systems, given the restrictions of the *Milliken* decision.[68]

Yet despite these overall trends *away* from a focus on the problem of segregation in urban schools, there were some efforts by community and civil rights advocates in a small number of metropolitan areas to address these problems through the creation of interdistrict school desegregation programs. These programs, which were the subject of our Ford Foundation study, were created as a way to address the growing isolation of students of color in central city schools by permitting students to transfer from city schools to suburban schools, or vice versa.

One such locale was Milwaukee, the site introduced at the beginning of the chapter. The interdistrict integration program there was known as Chapter 220, which was created via state legislation in 1975, and was later expanded as a result of a lawsuit filed by the Milwaukee school district. As one attorney we interviewed noted, Milwaukee was facing intense racial isolation at this time, isolation that had been created by both state action and suburban school district discrimination. At the time the lawsuit was filed, he noted that:

> About 97 percent of all African Americans in the Milwaukee metro area lived in the city of Milwaukee. Fewer than 3 percent at that time lived in the collective surrounding suburbs . . . When we brought the lawsuit, it was twenty-four suburban districts that we sued . . . We found that there were a number of things that the state and the suburban school districts had done to maintain their districts as kind of lily-white . . . We had a very thick memo that kind of laid out the evidence, and then we had smaller memos that discussed different pieces of it.

In 1987 the suit reached a limited decree settlement (meaning the plaintiffs could not go back to the court) between MPS, the state, and the suburban school districts, which resulted in the expansion of the Chapter 220 interdistrict integration program.[69]

Despite the victory in Milwaukee, in most metro areas school districts were simply unable legally or politically to get such programs adopted. Instead, the "technical school reform" era had begun—an era in which segregation became largely invisible in public policy, as reformers instead set out to find ways to fix segregated, high poverty, urban schools through educational reforms.[70] This technical reform approach was supported by the federal government, which provided extra funding to high-poverty schools. Such funds were welcome, in many cases, by financially strapped school systems.[71]

1990S TO THE PRESENT: EXTREME DIVISIONS AND DOUBLING DOWN ON TECHNICAL REFORMS

In the past several decades racial segregation has remained severe in many contexts, and income segregation has grown, as the wealthy and poor are living farther apart today than they were forty years ago. In an analysis of US Census data between 1970 and 2009, Stanford's sean reardon and Cornell professor Kendra Bischoff found that the number of people living in middle income neighborhoods declined significantly: "The proportion of families living in poor or affluent neighborhoods doubled from 15 percent to 33 percent, and the proportion of families living in middle income neighborhoods declined from 65 percent to 42 percent."[72] At the far extremes, they found, the proportion of people living in either "very wealthy" or "very poor" neighborhoods grew.

Further studies have found that families with different incomes live not only in different neighborhoods, but that they are increasingly residing in entirely different kinds of communities: while low income families are disproportionately concentrated into both cities and low income suburbs, higher income families are disproportionately concentrated into affluent suburbs.[73] While some gentrification is occurring in urban cores, it has affected only a minority of census tracts in most cities, causing segregation to re-emerge on a smaller scale in those cases.[74]

This growing spatial inequality by income is also reflected in school districts, as between-district segregation by income has increased by more than 15 percent from 1990 to 2010.[75] Research by University of Southern California professor Ann Owens suggests that demographic change is not merely reflected in district demographics, but that school districts are in fact *fueling* demographic change across metro areas, as higher income families use their resources (gained by rising income inequality) to move to—and separate themselves into—more affluent and higher performing districts.[76]

The mainstream educational policy world has largely ignored the growing segregation we have discussed and the related issues that result from concentrated poverty and structural racism, instead doubling down on the technical reform approach of prior decades that conceives of the problem of school failure as the fault of those within school systems: bureaucratic inefficiency, inadequate standards, inefficient resource allocation, and poor teaching. The solution, under this framing, is putting additional pressures on low performing schools via incentives and sanctions, and (though a lesser focus and somewhat weak in most instances) providing struggling schools with some supports.[77]

Such approaches were reflected in the three most recent reauthorizations of ESEA: the Improving America's Schools Act of 1994, the No Child Left Behind Act (NCLB) in 2002, and the Every Student Succeeds Act in 2016. Each of these reauthorizations sought to increase both educational standards and educators' work efforts by requiring schools to conduct annual testing. These laws required states to develop performance targets and implement sanctions on the lowest performing schools that failed to meet these targets. In recent years, federal funding was set aside for districts that turned around the lowest performing schools through a number of strategies, despite the fact that these did not have a strong research base, including reconstitution of the staff and closing and reopening the school under new management.[78] The idea of "turnaround" models suggests that if educators just have greater will or capacity, they could improve—it is just a matter of aligning the incentives in the right direction to cause this to happen.[79]

Accountability policies frame the problem of low performance in a way that overlooks the broader trends we have discussed. In this construction, the problem of low performance lies primarily *within* school systems. This perspective was also reflected in the expansion of market-based school-choice policies in the 1990s and early 2000s, which included the adoption of charter school laws in forty-three states and the District of Columbia by 2016.[80] Charter laws were intended to free traditional schools from bureaucratic systems, allowing them to innovate and compete with public schools, thereby forcing overall systemic improvement.[81] Open enrollment school-choice laws were also enacted by nearly all fifty states during this time to encourage districts to compete with each other.[82] Some started calling for portfolios for schools in urban districts, based upon market ideas in an effort to diversify the types of options available to families and reduce the influence of district central offices on individual schools.[83]

Returning to Milwaukee, we see that these approaches focusing on improvement via incentives and sanctions did not have the intended effects on traditional public schools. Indeed, research has largely concluded that NCLB did not significantly reduce achievement gaps.[84] In Milwaukee, the distribution of "failing schools" is closely linked to the segregation we have described above.[85] In figures 2.1 and 2.2 we show where the low performing schools are located using maps that indicate poverty (figure 2.1) and racial concentration (figure 2.2).[86] As these maps show, nearly all of the SIFI schools are located in census tract areas that are 41–100 percent poverty and in census tracts that are 41–100 percent African American or 41–100 percent Hispanic.

Given where things stand today in Wisconsin, there is little evidence that the technical reforms have had the desired effects. Indeed, these policies may have even exacerbated the issues given the growth in segregation as schools became labeled as failures and more people fled the system for other options.

Further, our research found that the free market, interdistrict open enrollment policy in Wisconsin, which allowed students to transfer between school districts regardless of the impact on racial demographics, had the effect of undermining the efforts toward integration by allowing whites to flee Milwaukee to suburban schools, taking the spaces in suburban schools that should have been set aside for students of color under the interdistrict integration program, Chapter 220.[87] As one of our interviewees noted of the conflicts between the Chapter 220 and the open enrollment programs: "[We have the Chapter 220] policy to promote integration in the metropolitan area, but then we've got this other program that promotes segregation . . . it's been mostly whites who have open-enrolled out of the city of Milwaukee." Further, as a Milwaukee district administrator observed, the open enrollment program, by draining whites out of the city, has had consequences on segregation and political support for Milwaukee schools:

> and as a result of that, a lot of political capital actually goes with the kids because [of] the lack of investment on the part of the people who have, I would say, some influence. They utilize [open enrollment] as a tool to re-segregate schools, whereas I think [Chapter] 220 was a little different. I mean, I think the goal was basically to build some social capital between races and . . . I mean, I'm kind of a [Chapter] 220 fan. I think it's a wonderful option for families who value diversity in their households. But now certainly I think Open Enrollment was totally different in my mind.

In addition to the political and social shifts created by the open enrollment program, the Milwaukee region's school choice programs as a collective (charters, open enrollment, and vouchers) have contributed to a decline in financial resources for Milwaukee schools, as the funding follows the students to the receiving schools. At the same time, the Milwaukee schools have been left serving the highest-needs students, as the same school district administrator in Milwaukee noted:

> You know, one of the big challenges here is that the reality . . . when these kids go to these places [through vouchers or charters or open enrollment], the special education kids don't go, unless they're the high incidence exceptionality. I mean, I keep all the kids who are special ed, I keep all the kids who are English language learners, limited English

FIGURE 2.1

Milwaukee Metro: Schools Identified for Improvement (SIFI) and percent of individuals under 18 years old in poverty by census tract

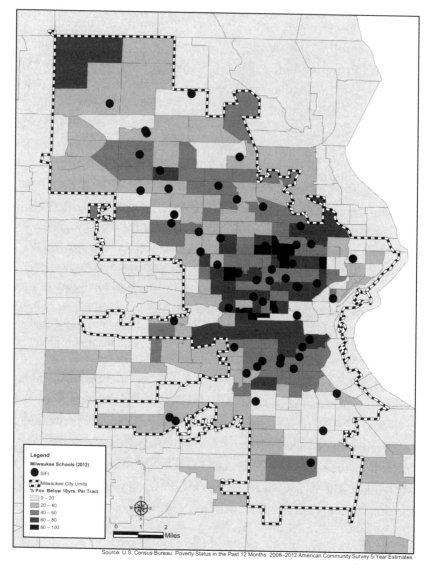

Source: U.S. Census Bureau. Poverty Status in the Past 12 Months: 2008–2012 American Community Survey 5-Year Estimates.

FIGURE 2.2

Milwaukee Metro: Schools Identified for Improvement (SIFI) and percent Black and Latino/a residents by census tract

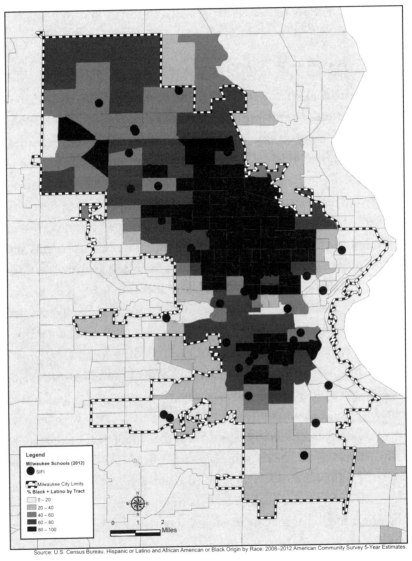

Source: U.S. Census Bureau. Hispanic or Latino and African American or Black Origin by Race: 2008–2012 American Community Survey 5-Year Estimates.

speaking, so those are your high-dollar kids . . . Even with vouchers none of them get lucky enough to make the lottery, can you imagine that? (sarcastically) They don't . . . I know it's Open Enrollment, but none of them ever get picked. What a coincidence! In 20 years none of them ever make it (sarcastically).

THE POLITICS OF THE MISDIAGNOSIS OF FAILURE

While individuals on the ground in Milwaukee and other locales in our study have worked hard to reduce inequities related to educational access and opportunity, often against strong political and educational pressures, the policy and political environments have often worked against them. While districts, states, and the federal government construct failure as an internal problem to schools that requires technical reform solutions, the growth in between-district segregation by income and persistent segregation by race has had serious implications for school systems and educational opportunity: curtailing access to diverse learning environments; limiting access to resources for students in lower income districts; and causing a competition over resources and status that has led to dysfunctional opportunity hoarding on the part of affluent families who advocate for advantages for only their children.[88]

Nowhere were these dynamics more evident than in Omaha, Nebraska, when, in June of 2005, the superintendent and school board voted to merge the urban Omaha Public School District with parts of several suburban school districts, so that the school district and city of Omaha limits would be the same (a policy called "One City, One School District"). The superintendent recalled when, at a community meeting in which he and other board members communicated the rationale for their decision to consolidate, an angry suburban mother told him why she was opposed to the merger:

At the break, after communicating the rationale, the process, and what we believed to be an outcome, a better outcome for all kids, a lady came up to me. She identified herself only as a person who lived in Elkhorn, very, very emotional, all shades of red, shaking her finger under my nose and saying, "You know what, my kids have ten crayons in Elkhorn, and it's really sad that kids in the Omaha Public Schools have five crayons. But you know what, if this thing called One City, One School District comes about, all kids are gonna have eight crayons, and over my dead body, my kid's gonna have ten crayons." And she marched off before I had an opportunity to say, why is it that we always assume that some kids are gonna have ten crayons, some kids are gonna have five; why don't we get about the business of ensuring that all kids have ten crayons; this is a city that's capable of doing anything. But she captured, for me, what this was truly all about, that we were moving away from a common good concept, to what's in it for me, how am I impacted, the individualized consumer approach to public ed.

This vignette helps illustrate how segregation has created a political geography of Us versus Them, an educational Not in My Back Yard that aligns with race and class, and that has fueled a hyper-localism that undermines needed efforts to address these problems on a regional scale. This helps to explain why the narrow, single-district, *within* education solutions are so appealing: they do not challenge the broader system of segregation and resource inequality that has driven these problems in the first place. In the rare cases when the policymakers have recognized and diagnosed the problem correctly (as we illustrate in the next chapter with a further exploration of interdistrict integration programs), these dynamics around localism and political geography place severe restrictions on the reforms that are adopted.

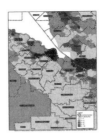

THREE

The Promise and Limits of Interdistrict Integration Programs

IN 1976, A GROUP of 170 African American parents, white parents, and students in Northern California filed a class-action lawsuit against local districts and the state of California under the name of a parent, Margaret Tinsley.[1] The lawsuit argued that students in the mostly black and low income Ravenswood School District, located in East Palo Alto, were denied an equal educational opportunity because of racial isolation created by the biased construction of school district boundary lines.[2]

After ten years of legal battles, the districts worked out a settlement that created an interdistrict integration program that was meant to both diversify the Ravenswood district and surrounding school systems and improve academic outcomes for minority students in Ravenswood. The goals of the original settlement were to "further equal education opportunities for all students in all respondent districts by 1) reducing minority racial isolation among or between the students of the respondent districts' elementary schools, 2) improving educational achievement in Ravenswood, and 3) enhancing inter-district cooperative efforts."[3]

The settlement is best known for the transfer program that came to be called the Tinsley program. Through the program, eight neighboring predominantly white suburban school districts (Redwood City, Menlo Park, Las Lomitas, Woodside, Portola Valley, Belmont, San Carlos, and Palo Alto) were required to enroll a small number of Ravenswood students, ranging from 5 to 60, each year.[4] The plan also called for the construction of a new "model school" in Ravenswood that was designed to strengthen the district and potentially attract students from the surrounding suburbs. Since the new school never materialized, Tinsley has always operated as a one-way program for Ravenswood students to attend schools in the surrounding suburbs. Once placed, a Ravenswood student is enrolled in the receiving district through graduation and attends high school in either the Sequoia Union High School District (the high school district for most of the participating districts, including East Palo Alto), or in the Palo Alto Unified School District.

For over five decades, interdistrict integration policies like the Tinsley program have been operating in major metropolitan areas in all regions of the country, making them one of the oldest but also least well-known types of school choice policies. Unlike newer charter school and voucher policies, interdistrict integration policies are specifically designed to promote racial and economic integration across district lines. At the time of our study (from 2008 to 2012), we identified interdistrict integration programs operating in thirteen metropolitan areas in ten states, although two of the programs have since been phased out. While they all focus on integration, they vary in length of history, key design features, size, and other important facets. The first was created in the 1960s in Rochester, New York, during the time of the race riots, with the most recent enacted by the Nebraska state legislature in 2007 in order to address inequities between school districts in the Omaha metropolitan area.

Today, interdistrict programs mostly exist as voluntary "cooperative agreements" between participating districts to address racial and/or socio-economic segregation.[5] In some programs, enrollment targets have been established via court settlements, while in other programs, students are accepted into districts based upon projections of the space available each year.[6] Enrollment goals vary across programs, with some focusing on race and others on socioeconomic status; admissions processes vary as well, with some using a lottery and others using a complex interview process. Most states provide receiving school districts with per-pupil state aid for students who transfer, but some also provide "hold-harmless funding" to districts that *send* students under these programs. A few programs explicitly incorporate funds and support for counseling, teacher training, and student supports, though this is not common. Unfortunately, no reliable numbers exist as to the number of students who have participated in or graduated from interdistrict integration programs, but we estimated, based on the most recent numbers from each program, that approximately 40,000 students participate each year in either urban-suburban interdistrict integration programs or interdistrict magnet schools.

From 2008 to 2012 we visited the sites of eight of these programs, conducting interviews with more than 100 educators, program administrators, attorneys, and civil rights advocates. The goal of our study was to understand the politics and implementation of these programs. What we found was both encouraging and discouraging. On the one hand, we heard many stories of hard-fought battles to get these off the ground. Establishing these programs was a significant victory in many contexts in light of the political and legal barriers (especially as a result of the 1974 *Milliken v. Bradley* decision) that advocates faced. We also heard about the positive benefits of these programs from students, teachers, and community members—benefits which are backed up by research.[7]

On the other hand, we found these programs are beset by a number of deep problems. We heard stories of conflicts between city and suburban school districts over the implementation of the programs, and in some cases resistance on all sides (from city residents and suburban residents). We also found a lack of consensus about the goals and purposes of the programs among teachers, administrators, and families, and in many instances, the programs have suffered from a serious lack of state and federal political support.[8]

We conclude that while these interdistrict integration programs have the potential to address segregation across school districts in a metropolitan area, they are, figuratively speaking, like small sandbags seeking to hold back the large tidal waters of inequality. They provide opportunities for some students, providing access to higher quality schools for many of those enrolled, but on the whole, they fail to alter the underlying system of relationships—segregation by race and income in schools and housing, as well as inequities in transit and economic development—that drives the inequality these programs are seeking to address.

In this chapter, we explore these tensions and further expand our argument that interdistrict integration programs are an important but insufficient policy strategy to address the dynamics of inequality in education. We begin with a case study of the Tinsley program, illustrating how political geography can work to undermine these programs. As we discussed in chapter 1, political geography refers to the ways in which both public policy and private actors have created racialized spaces over time. This political lens helps to show how city, school district, and neighborhood boundary lines have inscribed racial inequality into geographic space, setting up a cycle of inequality that privileges the suburbs and leaves urban school districts at a significant disadvantage in terms of resources, concentration of poverty, and political power. We then turn to the Rochester Urban-Suburban Interdistrict Transfer program (USITP), a case that illustrates how the localism we described earlier—the ways that individuals or communities work to promote their own interests legally and politically—creates conflicts that undermine these programs. The Rochester case illustrates how entrenched localism on the part of city and suburban residents, educators, and leaders hinders the potential of these programs in addressing equity.

HOW POLITICAL GEOGRAPHY LIMITS INTERDISTRICT INTEGRATION PROGRAMS

East Palo Alto is a small, 2.5 square mile city, with approximately 30,000 residents. It was the first planned community in San Francisco County, which later became San Mateo County. Founded in 1849 and named Ravenswood, it was attractive to settlers because of its location on the bay.[9] However, the port of Ravenswood did not have the same success as other ports, and the railroad made it obsolete.[10] Later merging with a town called Runnymede, the two towns became known as East Palo Alto (EPA).

By the late 1940s, EPA had 12,000 residents, was unincorporated, and its primary industry was agricultural with nurseries run by Italian and Japanese immigrants.[11] In the 1950s, the city of Menlo Park annexed an affluent and white part of EPA called Belle Haven which included about one-quarter of the EPA population and property value.[12] The loss of Belle Haven was a key point in EPA's history because it resulted in greater racial isolation.

While the residents of EPA subsequently tried to incorporate into their own municipality to stave off other annexations, they were not successful until decades later. In 1955, the widening of Highway 101 exacerbated the difficulties facing EPA, as the freeway displaced most of the existing business district and made certain areas less attractive to developers based upon their more isolated geography. This freeway expansion had a major impact, creating a class and racial divide between the areas east and west of the highway—namely between EPA and the more affluent

Palo Alto. Similar patterns were occurring all over the country as highways either completely removed minority communities or made them more geographically isolated. As an unincorporated town, EPA had little political power and, therefore, little voice in this highway decision.

EPA was a desirable location for African American migrants because of the low-cost housing and, unlike surrounding communities, lack of racially restrictive housing covenants, according to Michael Kahan, director of Urban Studies at Stanford.[13] He noted, "The spatial inequality between unincorporated East Palo Alto and its incorporated neighbors became more pronounced, and more racially marked, over the course of the postwar period." Indeed, the demographics shifted tremendously around this time, from being 72 percent white in 1960 to 61 percent black in 1970.[14] Although the freeway project set up a barrier between the African American and white communities, it also meant the town became known for its African American culture—important because this strengthened the community in many ways, but it also made it more "racially marked."[15] In addition, EPA had only about one-fifth of the sales tax revenue of the surrounding communities, which weakened its financial viability.[16]

It was during this postwar period that Ravenswood High School opened within the Sequoia Union High School District. The high school opened in 1958 with a primarily white student body (21 percent African American), but by 1970 had become 94 percent African American.[17] According to Cornell University history professor Russell Rickford, the school had, after white flight, become focused heavily on vocational education, and achievement had declined.[18] Concerned with the declining educational quality at Ravenswood High, a group of African American parents, spearheaded by Gertrude Wilks, organized in 1965 to form the advocacy group Mothers for Equal Education (MORE). Together with other activists, they demanded that Ravenswood High School be dissolved and that the children in the area be allowed to attend the neighboring district's predominantly white high schools. According to Rickford, "Wilks recognized . . . that outstanding faculty, curricula, and materials remained concentrated in white, middle-class schools, and she began developing a plan to connect East Palo Alto children with those resources."[19]

Unsuccessful in their appeals for the dissolution of Ravenswood High, the parents then organized what became known as "sneak outs," which involved finding white families in suburban school systems to house African American students four days per week so that they could attend school there. According to Rickford, over the course of two years nearly 200 students participated in the sneak outs. While the sneak outs faded after a few years, the program was formalized in 1968 as a small interdistrict transfer program between East Palo Alto and the Palo Alto district.

Yet even as the interdistrict program got started, some activists in EPA were growing disenchanted with integration, instead advocating for the creation of private, independent, community-based schools. According to Rickford's history, "East Palo Alto organizers embraced community control as an alternative to desegregation's 'destruction of self-esteem.'"[20] There was also a ballot initiative to change EPA's name to Nairobi, as a way to honor its African heritage. As Rickford describes, the name East Palo Alto suggested a colony subordinate to Palo Alto, while Nairobi symbolized black autonomy and African identity. The ballot measure, which was defeated, represented the ongoing push and pull between separatism and integration in this and other communities.

During this time, Ravenswood High School's enrollment continued to decline, and by 1976, the school was closed as a result of low enrollment and financial issues. While some African Americans were pushing for the dissolution of the school because of low quality programs, others felt that the closing of the school was a blow to Ravenswood's community identity and an important moment in the district's history. As an administrator describes:

> When you take a step back and you look at what's happened over time to East Palo Alto, there was a high school that was a Sequoia Union District high school in East Palo Alto, Ravenswood High, probably until the early 70's, and that was a really important part of the East Palo

Alto community. And then Sequoia had to decide—they had to close several high schools—and they closed San Carlos High School and they closed Ravenswood, and that's why the East Palo Alto kids go to Carlmont [in another town] because Carlmont stayed open. But there's no . . . you know a high school brings a lot of identity to a community and I think brings an anchoring and a grounding, and they don't have that.

A few years after the school's closure, the city of EPA finally successfully incorporated in 1983. However, it did not have enough revenue to survive, with limited commercial capacity—primarily known for its landfill, hazardous materials recycler, and pesticide plant,[21] indicating that the city was a victim of environmental racism as well.

Soon after incorporation, in 1986, the Tinsley settlement was put into place, allowing students of color in Ravenswood to transfer to the mostly white elementary and middle schools in suburban districts nearby. This settlement had three main goals: to increase the number of minority students in the mostly white surrounding school districts, to improve the educational standards of Ravenswood itself, and to increase the interdistrict cooperation between Ravenswood and the other districts.[22]

The Tinsley program currently accepts applicants in kindergarten through second grade. The participating suburban districts make spaces available for Ravenswood students based upon the size of their student populations at the time of the settlement. The allotted seats in each suburban district have not changed since 1986. As one administrator pointed out, the allocations determined in the 1980s have resulted in a negative impact on Ravenswood's enrollment over time because the Ravenswood district's enrollment has declined over the years due to demographic change and transfers to charter schools. Referring to seats set aside in suburban schools, the administrator notes:

It is actually a flat nominal number, it's not a percentage, and it's been a difficult thing for Ravenswood because those numbers were set in 1986 when Ravenswood's enrollment was much higher. So the total number of kids leaving the district was a smaller fraction of the total number of kids in the district in 1986 than it is now.

Under the settlement's provisions, the receiving districts are mandated to enroll Ravenswood students each year. Yet according to our interviews, there has been mutual distrust between Ravenswood and the suburban districts about the program and enrollment processes: Ravenswood administrators feared suburban districts would siphon off the highest-achieving students, while suburban districts thought that Ravenswood would use the program to push out the highest-needs students into their districts.

The only known study, to date, of the impact of the program on academic outcomes, by Kendra Bischoff, provides mixed evidence for these concerns.[23] On the one hand, Bischoff found that parents who applied to have their children admitted to the program were not more privileged in terms of household income and education: "The descriptive statistics suggest that the applicants are not vastly more economically advantaged or educated than similar adults in their neighborhoods. In fact, the applicant household is considerably poorer than the average household in the district, with 20 percent of neighborhood households reporting incomes of less than $30,000, compared to 52 percent of applicants" to the program.[24] On the other hand, she also found that applicant families were more likely to be fluent in English, have smaller household sizes, and be headed by a married couple.

In addition to the concerns about admissions, administrators we interviewed expressed skepticism as to whether the program is achieving its original mission in integrating schools within the region. Indeed, despite the settlement, the Ravenswood School District continues to exist as a majority minority district: 79 percent Hispanics/Latinx, 10 percent African American/Black, 9 percent Pacific Islander and 2 percent other races/ethnicities.[25] At the time of the settlement, 70 percent of students in Ravenswood were eligible for free or reduced-price meals, but rather than alleviating this high level of low income students in the district, the percentage has increased to 95 percent of students eligible for free or reduced-price meals as of the 2013/14 school year.[26]

Thus, while the small number of students who participate in the Tinsley program have access to heavily resourced schools, the Ravenswood district itself is as racially and socioeconomically isolated as ever. This core flaw in the program was in part due to the compromise that was struck in the settlement, allowing the white suburban districts to continue to exist in exchange for receiving transfer students. As one interviewee noted, the reason the suburbs agreed to the program in the first place was the threats of unification of all districts in the area:

> I believe that part of the issue is that because we [all elementary school districts in the area] are not a unified school district, that what was going to happen is it was likely that the judge was going to unify everybody and say, "instead of being eight or nine districts—eight feeding into one—we're going to make you one district." And I think that's why people settled, and, you know, I think maybe for educational outcomes for certain communities this has turned out well, but I think maybe from . . . if you're really worried about the larger social issues, and segregation or integration, probably should have unified, right? And so all we did was basically settle for something that says, "well, this will be good enough," but it's not good enough from an integration perspective.

Thus, the political geography placed severe limits on the remedy that was ultimately adopted, in that the power mostly resided in the white districts outside of Ravenswood, thereby limiting the positive impact of the settlement on Ravenswood students in particular. In essence, by creating this program the districts basically agreed to maintain the political structure as is, and in many ways exacerbated the racial and economic isolation of the Ravenswood community. Another administrator told us that when some suburban superintendents periodically raise questions about the settlement and wonder why it continues, the conversation always circles around to the potential legal threat of unifying all districts.

While the settlement was successful in getting affluent suburban schools to accept transfers, the program never ended up being a two-way program as was originally intended. As mentioned, there was a new school that was to be constructed in Ravenswood to attract suburban residents, but this never moved forward. Further, virtually no suburban students elected to transfer into the other Ravenswood schools. This has meant that Ravenswood has only lost students under the program and has become more racially isolated over time.

Much of the story of Tinsley focuses on the 1970s and 1980s, but in the last two decades the community—along with the Bay Area more broadly—has undergone tremendous changes, with growing inequality between East Palo Alto and surrounding communities. This has had the effect of exacerbating many of the issues the settlement was designed to resolve. In the late 1990s East Palo Alto, as a majority African American and lower income community in a more affluent and white area, faced a challenging situation. In an effort to spur economic development, the city council voted to redevelop a core part of the African American business district, known as Whiskey Gulch, voting "to demolish the city's primary retail district and to build in its place a five-star hotel and 451,000 square feet of class-A office space."[27] As Stanford Urban Studies director Kahan points out, there was a sad irony in this vote by the predominantly African American city council: "the city gave up a historic strip of minority-owned businesses [called Whiskey Gulch] in order to ensure the continued independent existence of a majority-minority city."[28] Ultimately, the city leaders realized that the current industries were not sustainable.

While outsiders saw EPA largely as a place of violence, crime, and drugs, for many others it was a diverse and vibrant community. Its prior unincorporated status and racially diverse population, however, excluded it from capital that would go toward economic development compared with other communities in the area that had prominent white power elites in leadership positions. In essence, its lack of political power historically, a result of having been unincorporated and geographically isolated, required additional steps so that it could sustain itself. This led to the decision to essentially give up key aspects of the EPA community to gain from the economic development investments in the region.

In the 2000s, the community continued to change as the district became majority Latinx, while at the same time there was an influx of more wealthy residents to the south bay as the technology boom in the Bay Area pushed families further and further out. These trends are illustrated in figures 3.1 and 3.2.

As the tech boom made land very costly, East Palo Alto suddenly became desirable to developers. However, the community tried to maintain restrictions on that growth so that EPA residents would benefit, prompting Facebook to commit to invest $20 million toward affordable housing, economic opportunity and tenant assistance in EPA (and Menlo Park) as part of its expansion into the area, and Amazon to promise to provide employment specialists to link residents with jobs at its new 1,300-employee office space.[29] As reporter Dara Kerr noted:

> East Palo Alto serves as a stark illustration of the growing divide caused by the tech boom. The Palo Alto side of the creek is flush with tech money—and it's not unusual for people to throw down millions for a single-family home—while nearly a fifth of East Palo Alto residents live below the poverty line. With the tech industry raising the cost of living and pushing folks out of other cities, East Palo Alto is one of the latest communities to attempt the balance between gentrification and preserving its roots.[30]

As home prices rose, many current EPA residents could no longer afford their homes; with 18 percent of the population at or below the poverty line, they were not reaping the same economic benefits. As a result of predatory lending, approximately 2,200 of the 6,600 single family homes went into foreclosure, and a developer bought up many rental properties and raised rents, forcing many long-standing residents out of the community.[31]

The redevelopment and infusion of wealth across the broad geographic area has, however, not had an impact on the Ravenswood School District. The isolation of the Ravenswood district remains, and additional policy strategies are needed to address the deeply entrenched structural inequities.

This is not to say there were no benefits from the program: in fact, Bischoff's study of the Tinsley program found that participating students have been able to reap some academic benefits, especially in the areas of science and history.[32] However, the study also found that because students had to endure challenges, including long bus rides, their opportunities for forming social ties were quite limited.

As this case study shows, the political geography of the Ravenswood area has resulted in the deepening isolation of students of color in East Palo Alto that was not ameliorated by the interdistrict transfer program that resulted from the Tinsley lawsuit. This is largely due to the fact that the decisions around housing, economic development, transportation, and other areas over time basically cordoned off the community of East Palo Alto and exacerbated the already difficult situation facing students in Ravenswood's schools. Though many suburban school leaders raised concerns about the effect of the Tinsley program, they also were complicit in maintaining its structure as a one-way program from Ravenswood to the suburbs in spite of the fact that they knew it was having limited impact on integration and, by many accounts, a negative impact on Ravenswood itself. The district is currently facing a financial crisis due to the steady decline in enrollments, and faces a possible state takeover as a result.[33] Unless the power dynamic shifts—which might happen given the demographic changes occurring in the area, although it is possible the communities of color will also be pushed out with these changes—greater efforts to tackle educational inequities in light of these historical patterns seem unlikely.

FIGURE 3.1

Tinsley program districts (CA): Percent Black and Latinx residents in school districts by census tract

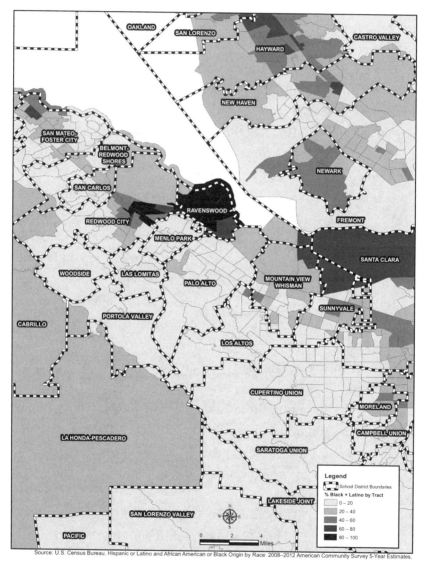

Source: U.S. Census Bureau. Hispanic or Latino and African American or Black Origin by Race: 2008–2012 American Community Survey 5-Year Estimates.

Note: Tinsley program districts are Ravenswood, Redwood City (no longer in the program), Menlo Park, Las Lomitas, Woodside, Portola Valley, Belmont-Redwood Shores, San Carlos, and Palo Alto.

FIGURE 3.2

Tinsley program districts (CA): Percent of individuals under 18 years old in poverty in school districts by census tract

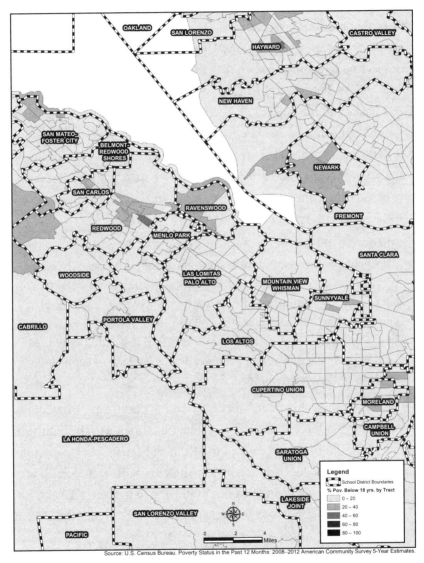

Source: U.S. Census Bureau. Poverty Status in the Past 12 Months: 2008–2012 American Community Survey 5-Year Estimates.

Note: Tinsley program districts are Ravenswood, Redwood City (no longer in the program), Menlo Park, Las Lomitas, Woodside, Portola Valley, Belmont-Redwood Shores, San Carlos, and Palo Alto.

HOW LOCALISM INTERVENES TO UNDERMINE INTERDISTRICT PROGRAMS

We next turn to Rochester, which is a case that illustrates how the localism that political geography engenders can also work to undermine interdistrict integration programs. Upstate New York is probably not the first place people think of when they think of multigenerational poverty in the United States. Yet Rochester, a midsize city situated between the Great Lakes and the Finger Lakes, once a thriving area and a home base for Kodak and Xerox, has become a poster child for the stark inequities that exist across metro areas in the United States, with a declining population and the loss of major industries—including Kodak, Xerox, and Bausch and Lomb—to suburbs or other areas outside of upstate New York. As a recent report notes:

> Almost one-third of the population lives below the poverty line. Of these, half live in extreme poverty—meaning that the household income is half of the federal poverty level. But most shocking is the fact that one out of every two children in Rochester lives in poverty . . . In the area known as "the Crescent," more than 60 percent of residents live in poverty. This extreme concentration of poverty manifests itself in limited local employment, housing blight, food deserts, and the isolation of the residents of these neighborhoods.[34]

Important to the Rochester story is that other parts of Monroe County are thriving, with recent federal and state investments in the high-tech industry of photonics, extensive growth in the exurbs, and numerous schools recognized for their excellence. These stark differences map very closely to race/ethnicity and income, as illustrated in figures 3.3 and 3.4. Rochester provides but one example of many cities across the United States that demonstrate these same patterns.

For years the city's school system, the Rochester City School District (RCSD), has been heavily segregated from the larger county. The city school district, which is comprised of students who are 90 percent nonwhite and 91 percent economically disadvantaged,[35] is surrounded by predominantly white and higher income suburbs. Indeed, Monroe County, in which Rochester is situated, is 77 percent white, with 15 percent living in poverty (compared with 33 percent in the city of Rochester), according to the US census.[36] These stark inequities are reflected in the district's performance: the district has a four-year graduation rate of 48 percent, the lowest of the five big-city districts in the state, and has struggled with meeting state performance standards: just under 8 percent of students in grades 3–8 are considered proficient in ELA and math, as compared with 25 to 76 percent in the surrounding districts.[37]

Rochester's history around race has caused deep scars and divisions in the community. Further, as local journalist Mark Hare argues, there seems to be very little political will to reverse the inequities caused by segregation or the challenges resulting from concentrated poverty in the city center. In describing the cold and extremely negative responses to talk of integration, he highlights an "us versus them" mentality that has resulted over decades of conflict, leaving little attempt to address these regional inequities: "In Monroe County, too many people have become comfortable with walls between city and suburbs, white and black, affluent and poor."[38]

Despite these divisions, there *has* been some attempt to address these issues in education. As mentioned previously, the Rochester metro area is home to the oldest interdistrict integration policy, known as the Urban-Suburban Interdistrict Transfer program (USITP). The USITP emerged in the aftermath of racial unrest in July 1964 that resulted in the declaration of a state of emergency and the use of the National Guard to quell tensions.[39]

A former USITP administrator involved with the program since its inception recalled that, around the same time, the Commissioner of Education sent out a directive as to how districts were going to deal with the problem of minority group isolation. As the administrator noted, "Just

FIGURE 3.3

Rochester, NY Metro: Percent Black and Latinx residents in school districts by census tract

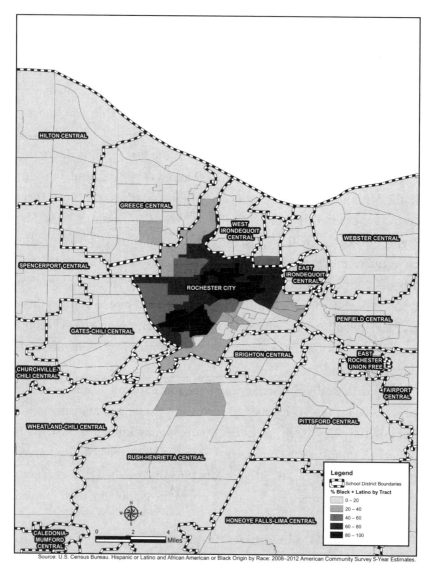

Source: U.S. Census Bureau. Hispanic or Latino and African American or Black Origin by Race: 2008–2012 American Community Survey 5-Year Estimates.

FIGURE 3.4

Rochester, NY Metro: Percent of individuals under 18 years old in poverty in school districts by census tract

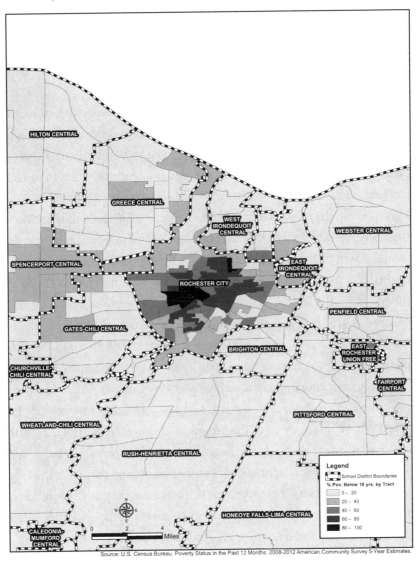

Source: U.S. Census Bureau. Poverty Status in the Past 12 Months: 2008-2012 American Community Survey 5-Year Estimates.

about every district in the suburbs responded they didn't have a problem, because they had no minority group students." West Irondequoit, outside of Rochester, initiated the local response to the state, arguing in a local newsletter, "No suburb exists in a vacuum. It is part of a metropolitan whole. The daily life of each citizen, whether urban or suburban, is closely intertwined, and the awareness of this interdependency should be a part of our educational structure."[40]

That year the West Irondequoit district allowed twenty-five students from the city to transfer to its schools, and several other districts soon joined in. USITP has always operated as a voluntary interdistrict choice program, which in some ways has allowed it to endure, while in others has limited its scope and impact as discussed in more detail below.

At present, the program involves approximately 700 students who live in the Rochester City School District and transfer to thirteen of the eighteen school districts in Monroe County. The current formal policies regarding selection and eligibility in the USITP state that, in order to enroll in the program, the student must be a resident of the city of Rochester and enrolled in grades K–8. Until recently, the program required that students were a minority as defined by the State of New York Education Department, but this was removed as a requirement. Parents must commit to attending mandatory parent meetings with program administrators (two per year) and must pay fifteen dollars into a scholarship fund for USITP graduates. When applying to the program, the parents may not designate a desired district or school, but instead apply to the program at large. The aid from the Rochester district follows the student from the city to the suburbs, which results in a net gain to participating districts, as city funding is significantly higher than their own state per-pupil aid, though each district has to pay back a small amount per student for administrative support.

While some argue that the program is useful in providing low income students of color in Rochester with access to educational programs in suburban schools, others have noted that the suburban communities limit the potential of the program through the application and selection process. Part of the problem is the difficulty parents have in finding out about the program: USITP is not advertised to students or families through print or other media; rather, families usually find out about it by word of mouth, either from other participants, graduates, guidance counselors, or teachers. This can have the effect of limiting applications to those that are the most connected to the school and/or existing networks. In addition, the suburban districts have a great deal of say in the selection of students. Each parent must submit a formal application to the USITP program for each of their children, after which program administrators acquire report cards and test scores from the student's Rochester school, or from the charter or private school the student attends (the program is open to residents of Rochester and is not limited to public school students only). After this first round of screening, those applicants selected to move forward—both the student and parent—must be interviewed by suburban school administrators, who decide if the student is accepted to a suburban school. More than 1,000 applications are submitted each year, but less than 10 percent are accepted.

One of the administrators involved in our study talked about some of the screening practices in his district. As this quote illustrates, although the program is not designed to take only a certain type of kid, the screening that occurs, along with possible biases around behavior, "motivation," and "home support," often means that the program has accepted students who were performing fairly well academically, and who exhibited certain behavioral characteristics:

> I think what I'm looking for are red flags more than anything . . . This is a big change for kids, to come to a whole different school and get settled in and ride the bus and, you know, out of their neighborhoods, and all of that, so you want someone that looks kind . . . that can have some self-confidence and good attendance, seems to be motivated, you know, they don't always have to be all A students, but out of a scale of one to four, you wouldn't take someone that all had ones either . . . I guess it's like you're looking at the whole picture, and attendance is . . . I don't know if I said

that, you know, if they've missed fifty days then that's not good, that usually means that there's not a good parent support to miss that many days.

For their part, suburban administrators viewed this selection process as a needed strategy to negotiate the tension they feel between their desire to accept students, and suburban parents' willingness to support this program only if it does not impact their own children's opportunities, or at least their perceptions of opportunities in these highly competitive communities. For example, we were told stories of parents who said they did not want USITP students taking their children's spots in gifted and talented programs or on sports teams, and also of parents who expressed concerns that the program would lead to the need to pay for academic supports for nonresident children, and that this money would be taken away from some other area that would benefit their own children. An administrator talked about how even in a community that generally supports the program there can be a lot of racist stereotypes.

> They will automatically assume that "those kids" that come in, and I use that term because that's the term I hear, that they're kids that are involved in fights and drugs, and things like that, because they associate that with the city, and often they are the best kids that we have in the building. It's about stereotypes and misperceptions and biases and bigotry, and all those things wrapped in, and small-town thinking.

Another form of suburban resistance is a limit on the number of spaces made available to city residents. Unlike the Tinsley program, which determined the number of spots that had to be made available in each district in the original settlement, and which remains the same each year, the number of available seats each year in Rochester is determined at the building or district level (or a combination of the two). Suburban administrators usually review approximately 100 applications for two to three openings in a grade, and in some grades, they offer no spaces at all. Once a student is admitted, he or she is allowed to continue in that school district through graduation if the student does not move out of the city, but can be removed involuntarily if academic or social expectations are not met. If a student leaves the program (voluntarily or involuntarily), or does not choose to accept the opening when it is offered, the spot remains unfilled. One administrator discussed what she saw as the challenges around admitting students, and the expectation in their communities that a city school student won't cost the district in terms of larger class sizes, extra supports like special education services, etc. Indeed, this strict screening criteria resulted in one parent actually having to decline the services her child was entitled to, just so that student could access opportunities in a suburban school through the program. As the administrator noted:

> We've had the luxury of small class sizes. So if I already had 24 or 25 in a class, I wouldn't take anymore . . . So I look to see where I can take kid[s], and for a few years I was taking them more in the intermediate grades because I could look at their New York state work, because sometimes you take them in the younger grades, and if they end up being . . . needing special education, they can't receive it here, they have to go back to their home district. And you can't always tell from an application, you know, if someone has special needs because that evolves in your little kids. And that happened one time where one of the children clearly had a learning disability, and the parents wanted him to stay here so much that they would not put him in special education, because they didn't want him back in the city, so we kept him and it was quite a dilemma because you can't give him the services, but you have to do some adapting.

Another educator expressed frustration about the ongoing conversations around having city kids in the suburban schools. As he says, educators are often not used to educating a diverse student body, and he felt that this needed to be addressed through professional development and other strategies—in terms of educating the educators so they were better prepared to teach in culturally relevant and appropriate ways—but he then contradicted himself as to whether this was even necessary as he talked about the fact that any teacher should be able to teach any child:

A lot of it is educating the teachers, the counselors, even the administrators . . . It's surprising to me that kids coming from the city is still some big deal . . . So if you're a teacher, as far as I'm concerned, and I might be naïve about this, you should be able to teach anybody. That's what I think. You got certified, you're a teacher, so if you've got a black kid, an Asian kid, a Hispanic kid, and they're all regular education kids . . . where they come from, what their makeup and their family is [shouldn't matter]. If they're there you should be able to teach them.

As is clear, while this particular administrator thought that the issue of race needed to be confronted with teachers, he took a more colorblind approach to addressing the diversity in the district, indicated by the stance that race should not matter. However, research has shown that this colorblind approach has the effect of cementing, rather than reducing, racial inequities within schools.[41]

Although in recent years there have been explicit attempts to expand the program into additional school districts in the county, including some more rural districts, the program still only serves a very small proportion of the 30,000 students in the Rochester district (about 2 percent). In addition, community conversations about program expansion have had strong racial overtones. In 2014, as the fiftieth-year anniversary of the program approached, the program drew attention in the local media, and there was an internal push by the USITP governing board to get more suburban districts to participate in the program. As a result of this push, six more districts joined the program.[42] However, not all of these districts joined because of concerns about equity—many were explicit that the additional resources attracted them to the program.

One of the suburban districts that was considering whether to join the program was frequently in the news around the decision. The district, which is five miles from Rochester, was considering adding a total of seventy-two students (beginning with eighteen) in a district of 3,700 that is 87 percent white. The district held public hearings about the decision, during which current students and alumni of the program shared their positive experiences. However, a small but vocal group of opponents of the program's expansion shared racist views of the city school students and their families—complaining that the transfer students would corrupt the community, that they didn't work hard enough, and other statements with racial overtones. One current USITP eleventh grader who spoke at the open meetings said she wasn't prepared for the comments from the community and noted that it was "hurtful and discouraging" to hear such racist remarks.[43] One of the local writers noted that everyone seemed to think the district was a special place but "the question was whether that specialness should be protected or shared"[44]—this is localism at work. As a result of the heated meetings, an alumna of the program wrote an article in the paper entitled "I'm Sorry, Future Spencerport Urban-Suburban Students." In this she directed her thoughts as a letter to the future students, stating: "I'm sorry that you will be walking into a district that unabashedly made it clear they find no value in your existence and that they do not want you in school with their children. I'm sorry that you will have the task of learning in an environment so charged, for no real reason other than the misplaced fear of a few very vocal residents."[45] Of course, not all residents in these suburban communities share these racist views of students living in the city, but both racist views and structural racism reinforce these inequities and limit the program's reach.

While these descriptions of how localism plays out in terms of the ways that suburban communities exercise their power to constrain these programs, it is also important to highlight how localism plays out through the resistance of city stakeholders. In fact, the original program was two-way, with transfers of students going both into the city and out to the suburbs. However, one of the earliest administrators told us that over time, suburban families only wanted to attend the more coveted schools in the city, and that city families and administrators did not want to give up those spaces to suburban kids. With a few exceptions, city administrators have had a weak connection to the interdistrict transfer program—while the suburban superintendents participate on the governing board, the city school superintendent rarely does. Further, parents of city school students often resist the urban-suburban program because it means a loss of middle-class parents,[46] despite the fact that many of these same parents seek out the more exclusive magnet programs or charter schools in the city.

The issues of educational inequities in the Rochester area is not a new topic, nor is the resistance that emerges when possible strategies are proposed. In the early 2000s, the former mayor was running for county executive, and many believe that the fact that he brought up the possibility of a countywide school district cost him the job, as his ideas were met with fierce opposition,[47] a common response of suburban residents that is linked to the politics of localism. As one stakeholder said, "To be very blunt, racism and ignorance are the two main reasons why we don't have a countywide system, plus economic self-interest."

Since 2013, a grassroots faith-based group has been trying to gain traction around the creation of an interdistrict magnet school, and recently the Rochester City School District voted to support this, but broader efforts, beyond one school, remain scarce, and political support, despite five years of effort, remains tenuous. In parallel, an antipoverty initiative was spearheaded by the former head of the United Way and a state representative in 2014, and then supported by Governor Cuomo at the state level in 2015. It was meant to focus on both Rochester and Monroe County, and had education as one of its eight "pillars." Although one of the four education-related recommendations of the group included efforts toward "racial, socioeconomic integration," no attention has been given to this area since the report was released in September 2015.[48] The group's recommendations around housing also took a regional approach, and these were not tackled either. Instead, the initiative (and community leaders engaged in it) has focused primarily on two areas: workforce development through adult career mentoring, and place-based investments in one neighborhood through the Purpose Built Communities organization.[49]

THE LIMITS OF INTERDISTRICT INTEGRATION PROGRAMS

While interdistrict integration programs like those in Rochester and East Palo Alto have enabled thousands of students, over decades, to cross district lines, and have fostered relationships between urban and suburban communities that had not previously existed, none have been able to address the inequities between districts that they were created to solve. Indeed, in a dissenting opinion to a lawsuit brought by a white student against the Rochester program decades ago, one of the judges noted the failure of the program in reducing racial isolation, one of its primary goals, based upon the length of time and the number of students involved.[50]

From our research, we found that both political geography and localism have worked in ways that undermine these programs. Recall the metaphor we used earlier, likening these programs to sandbags staving back the waves of challenges facing these urban areas, challenges that result from policies that have punished communities rather than supporting regional equity. While an attempt to reduce segregation, interdistrict integration programs often end up being inequitable for the students and for the city school systems themselves, and they rarely address the challenges within cities and the long-standing inequities that motivated the creation of the programs in the first place. The core problem with these programs is that they do not address the underlying system of relationships—the competitive dynamics and segregation between cities and suburbs that we referred to in chapters 1 and 2—that have not only created but also sustained these inequities over time. In a number of places, like Milwaukee for example, these programs were viewed as part of a broader strategy—sort of a first step in broader regional change. Indeed, an African American attorney in our study noted that it was really just meant to be a "stopgap" measure to get things "off the ground," but then the idea was to have African American students transferring to the suburbs and white students transferring into the city, followed by African American families moving to the suburbs and white families relocating to the city. These programs were often considered the starting point, but the political dynamics in these communities led them to be the only policy solution used and, in the end, they just aren't strong enough.

While interdistrict programs have provided opportunities to many students of color, and at times prompted important discussions around equity, there are broader issues and structures that must be addressed—both in the programs and more broadly—to bring about metropolitan/regional equity between city and suburban schools. Indeed, from our research it is clear that efforts to address segregation and educational inequality through these narrow mobility programs alone will never be adequate. As we discuss in the following chapters, comprehensive educational policy strategies geared toward regional equity, as well as strategies that incorporate other areas like housing, transportation, and economic development, are warranted and even more necessary than ever as these inequities worsen. To delineate and learn from comprehensive regional approaches both within and outside of education, we turn to some of the bolder approaches in urban policy in chapter 4.

FOUR

Cross-Sector Regional Initiatives in Urban Policy

THE INTERDISTRICT SCHOOL integration programs we described in chapter 3 have been limited in their ability to address inequality and segregation between school districts, in large part because they do not address the underlying systems of relationships that create those problems. In other words, the interdistrict integration programs fail to address the competitive relationships between school districts and between cities—dynamics which, when overlaid on patterns of economic and housing segregation, leave both low income school districts and cities segregated, isolated, and with few resources.

In some metro areas, there have been efforts to explicitly address these systems of relationships through regional approaches that seek to ensure coordination rather than competition across jurisdictions in a region and to address the underlying inequities. As Scott Bollens, professor of Planning, Policy and Design at the University of California at Irvine, writes of regionalism: "A basic premise of this perspective is that regions should be pursuing policies that reduce racial segregation, concentration of poverty, neighborhood distress, disproportionate exposure of the poor to environmental risk, and interjurisdictional inequality because these conditions undermine the economic competitiveness and overall well-being of a region."[1]

The Twin Cities of Minneapolis–St. Paul was one of the first metro areas to adopt such an approach. In 1967, the Minnesota state legislature created the first regional governing body in the country, the Met Council. The goal of the council was to address the inefficiencies and inequalities created by the existence of multiple, competing jurisdictions. When the council was created, then-governor Harold LeVander said the Council "was conceived with the idea that we will be faced with more and more problems that will pay no heed to the boundary lines which mark the end of one community in this metropolitan area and the beginning of another."[2]

Minneapolis–St. Paul's effort was part of a broader movement, led by moderate Republican governors in the late 1960s and early 1970s, to address the problems of imbalances across metropolitan areas.[3] As Myron Orfield writes, while these "good government" reformers "supported equity, it was with a hard-headed calculation of the costs of inequity and the destructive competition for development among municipalities in a region."[4] Similar reforms were adopted in Indianapolis and Portland, Oregon.[5] Over the following decades, in a series of initiatives, the Met Council in the Twin Cities began to address a number of issues regionally, including transit problems, tax base inequality between cities and suburbs, and the distribution of affordable housing across the region.

In this chapter, we consider regional approaches as a potential solution to the core problems we have laid out in this book: segregation, school failure, and inequality between schools and school districts. We describe both the history of these regional initiatives and the core elements of these programs. However, we also show a key weakness to these efforts:

the fact that these regional movements have not integrated education into their approaches, and have largely left the inequality between school districts untouched even though these are closely linked to many of the areas they target.

REGIONAL DILEMMAS, REGIONAL SOLUTIONS

One of the defining features of American political geography is the relatively large number of autonomous governmental units, such as municipalities, townships, and local school districts within metropolitan areas.[6] While this "geopolitical fragmentation"[7] is prevalent in all major US metropolitan areas, it is particularly notable in the older industrialized cities of the Northeast and Midwest.[8]

Metropolitan areas in the United States were not always divided into multiple, autonomous jurisdictions. As we noted in chapter 2, the phenomenon of fragmentation emerged during the mid-twentieth century, when the growing number of predominantly white and middle-class suburbs were granted powers of incorporation, with attendant taxing and revenue authority, by state legislatures.[9] As a result, suburbs and suburban school systems became independent political units that were largely able to detach themselves from the growing urban problems nearby.

Metropolitan areas with high levels of fragmentation tend to have political units (i.e., school districts, municipalities) that are not only more numerous but relatively smaller in size. Some argue that there are benefits to such configurations: smaller jurisdictions not only help to create and solidify community identity, but their small size means that they can more efficiently meet the preferences of individuals living within their borders.[10]

Yet there is also evidence that geopolitical fragmentation comes with serious social and political costs, contributing to fiscal disparities between locales and exacerbating racial and economic segregation across metropolitan areas.[11] In this perspective, concentrated poverty and suburban sprawl are two sides of the same coin: as metropolitan areas have experienced rapid development in outer-ring suburbs, it has caused central cities to slip into downward spirals.[12] These dynamics have resulted in "spatial disparities" with separate communities of concentrated poverty and wealth that reduce equality of opportunity, including educational and employment opportunities.[13] Perhaps most concerning is that, over time, generations of residents are living separately across racial and class lines, leading to spatial, racial, and social distance. Furthermore, as these divisions grow, not only do wealthier families no longer share the same public amenities and governmental agencies with lower income households, but stereotypes and distrust make it less likely that these citizens will favor longer-term investments that would reverse these trends.[14] As public policy professor Paul Jargowsky, who focuses on geography and segregation, points out, these patterns are not to be blamed on individual families or even developers but rather on the complex set of tax and zoning rules, development subsidies, and governmental fragmentation that allowed these patterns to flourish.[15]

Yet over the past several decades, reformers have proposed addressing these dynamics through policies aimed at increasing intergovernmental cooperation among local communities within metropolitan areas.[16] Regional solutions grow out of a recognition that existence of jurisdictional lines (such as city or school district boundary lines) results in a competition between communities that often leaves urban cores and inner-ring suburbs at distinct disadvantages with respect to economic growth and fiscal health, and also with respect to higher levels of racial segregation and concentrated poverty. As john powell observes, regional solutions that focus on regional equity shift the framework for urban policymaking: "regional or metropolitan equity offers policymakers a way to reconceptualize metropolitan areas for the common good of all residents, affluent or not. Instead of calling upon each locality to take responsibility only for itself, regionalism recognizes the entire area as a system of interdependent parts. The whole will prosper only if all parts are able to function."[17]

Calls for regional reform have been in existence since the late nineteenth century, when cities moved to annex outlying suburbs, or consolidate with them, in an effort to address inefficiencies generated by multiple governments in the same region. However, as we noted in chapter 2, beginning in the early twentieth century, city annexations were increasingly stopped by state legislatures as suburbs began to exert growing influence on state policy.[18]

Since that time, regional efforts have moved away from a focus on the politically difficult strategies of annexation and consolidation to a focus on coordination between cities in a metropolitan area. These regionalism efforts typically involve the creation of a governance structure consisting of representatives of localities across a region who are charged with solving regional problems or challenges in a number of areas. The efforts involve policy in varied domains, from transit to parks. We argue that, conceptually, these approaches show great promise. We use examples from Detroit, the Twin Cities, and Portland to illustrate the important federal, state, and local roles in promoting such solutions. While regional solutions are, at least in theory, politically less difficult than annexation or consolidation given the current legal constraints, we show in this chapter that addressing the core issues of segregation and resource inequity requires explicit attention to these matters.

THE FEDERAL GOVERNMENT ROLE IN PROMOTING REGIONALISM

The federal government was responsible for the first national wave of regional planning via the 1954 federal Housing Act, which required that planning grants be given only to regional agencies. This Act led many metropolitan areas to establish regional councils, originally termed Councils of Governments (COGs), which consisted of representatives from local jurisdictions across a region who came together for the purposes of common planning.

The very first COG was created in Detroit in 1954, and it has since served as a model for regional councils in other metropolitan areas.[19] The Detroit council was originally called the Supervisor's Inter-County Committee, and it consisted of a voluntary cooperative organization of county supervisors in the six-county area in Detroit.[20] According to a document written in 1956 describing this committee: "the Supervisor's Inter-County Committee is a means for making the county governmental units *that already exist* work more effectively. Another government layer is not being added to those we already have. The only thing new is that six counties are cooperating to solve common problems."[21]

In 1968 this committee was expanded to include additional members and renamed the South East Michigan Council of Governments (SEM-COG). The committee oversaw issues such as roads, water, sewage, and parks. Yet, despite the severe racial segregation that had grown between the city and suburban school systems in the Detroit metropolitan area by the late 1960s, education was not included as a regional issue to address by the SEMCOG council. Those advocates hoping to address segregation instead had to turn to the courts.

As a result, just two years after SEMCOG was created, Detroit became the site of the now famous school desegregation case, *Milliken v. Bradley*, that challenged patterns of metropolitan segregation between Detroit city and suburban school districts caused by school district boundary lines. The case was filed in 1970 by the Detroit branch of the NAACP, which claimed that Michigan state officials were responsible for the segregation between the predominantly black Detroit city school system and the surrounding white suburbs. The lawsuit sought to remedy this problem by proposing a metropolitan desegregation plan that involved both the city and suburban districts. The district court judge, Judge Stephen J. Roth, agreed with the NAACP's claims and in a 1972 ruling ordered the state to design a metropolitan plan to integrate city and suburban school systems. He also appointed a panel to come up with this interdistrict solution to Detroit's segregation problems. In his ruling, Judge Roth cited the existence of SEMCOG as proof that regional solutions to educational problems—and the overriding of school district boundaries as ordered in this decision—were justified:

> Local units of government in the metropolitan area have in many instances joined together for the purpose of providing better solutions to problems confronting them. In such instances various units of government have either disregarded local boundaries or have concluded that the problems were such as to call for a metropolitan solution. In some cases they have created overlay organizations. SEMCOG, recreational authorities, a metropolitan sewage system, SEMTA [Southeastern Michigan Transportation Authority], and the Detroit Water System are examples of these metropolitan approaches.[22]

The state appealed Judge Roth's metropolitan desegregation order to the US Supreme Court. In 1974, the US Supreme Court ruled in the 5–4 *Milliken* decision that a federal court could not impose an interdistrict plan to address de jure segregation occurring within one district (Detroit) when outlying suburban school districts were not found to be directly culpable. The court's majority argued that, in order to require a metropolitan desegregation remedy, plaintiffs must show proof of intentional discrimination on the part of suburbs or on the part of the state in drawing boundary lines.

Justice Thurgood Marshall condemned the decision in his dissent, arguing school district boundary lines served to solidify racial barriers when court decrees were limited to the city alone: "School district lines, however innocently drawn, will surely be perceived as fences to separate the races when, under a Detroit-only decree, [w]hite parents withdraw their children from the Detroit city schools and move to the suburbs in order to continue them in all-[w]hite schools."[23]

As Marshall predicted, the *Milliken* ruling effectively shut down efforts to integrate schools in metro areas outside the south, and after the

Milliken ruling, the issue of school segregation remained unaddressed in Detroit, both by the courts and by SEMCOG. Indeed, on education and on other equity issues, SEMCOG had relatively little power—in reality it could not force localities to do anything they did not want to do. However, it did have a symbolic role in promoting regional collaboration between the city and suburbs in the metro area.

Since the early 1970s, the number of regional councils like SEMCOG has increased, thanks in large part to federal grants that were given to councils for regional planning, particularly transit grants.[24] In 1957, there were fewer than 10 Councils of Governments in the country, but by 1972 there were more than 300, and by 1980, 660 existed.[25] One major factor behind the growth of COGs in the 1980s was the 1973 Federal Highway Act, which created funding for urban mass transit, and for the first time, authorized federal funding for Metropolitan Planning Organizations (MPOs) in every metro area with more than 50,000 residents.[26] Many COGs were designated as MPOs for their regions as a result of this legislation. They were strengthened in 1991 by federal transportation funding which required that urban areas have a designated MPO for creating regional transportation plans.[27] As a result of these efforts, MPOs are, as University of Minnesota law professor Myron Orfield notes, "the most widespread form of regional governance in the United States today."[28]

While the MPOs and COGs provide a means for coordination between cities and suburbs within a metropolitan area to address problems across a region, research has shown that, as currently structured, their power is especially limited on issues of regional equity. This is for several reasons: First, their review power centers largely on transit, water, and other infrastructure issues, and not on issues of housing and schools. Second, members of the councils are appointed, not elected, and representation is not based on population, leaving the body unaccountable to the public and with disproportionate suburban influence.[29] Third, as voluntary associations, the councils are unable to impose mandates, and they tend to shy away from controversial issues for fear that members may pull out of the organization.[30] Indeed, as political scientists Robert England, John Pelissero and David Morgan write, "COGs are notorious for avoiding politically sensitive problems that might involve social change, such as metropolitan approaches to low income housing and school desegregation."[31]

STATE AND LOCAL EFFORTS AT REGIONALISM: THE TWIN CITIES AND PORTLAND

Movements toward regional coordination have also taken place at the state and local levels. To date, two metro areas have successfully forged what could be considered strong regional solutions in urban policy, in contrast to the weaker structure of the MPOs and COGs described above.

As we noted earlier, the first strong regional government was formed in the Minneapolis–St. Paul region. The Twin Cities' regional government was created in 1967 when the state legislature established the Met Council, a seventeen-member regional council with control over growth planning, transit, infrastructure, and parks.[32] At the time, the legislature directed the council to:

> Prepare and adopt . . . a comprehensive development guide for the metropolitan area. It shall consist of a compilation of policy statements, goals, standards, programs, and maps prescribing guides for the orderly and economical development, public and private, of the metropolitan area. The comprehensive development guide shall recognize and encompass physical, social, or economic needs of the metropolitan area and those future developments which will have an impact on the entire area including but not limited to such matters as land use, parks and open space land needs, the necessity for and location of airports, highways, transit facilities, public hospitals, libraries, schools, and other public buildings.[33]

The Met Council was created, in part, as a response to the federal planning laws noted above. However, the Met Council was also created to help address local concerns around fragmented planning between the cities in the region. According to one written history: "The drive for the Council's creation was led by citizens and legislators. They saw the need for a regional body to deal with issues that transcended the boundaries of nearly 300 separate local units of government (7 counties, 188 cities and townships, and 22 special-purpose districts)."[34]

The seventeen members are appointed by the governor and represent geographic districts. These geographic districts do not overlap directly with municipalities; thus, the representatives do not solely represent municipalities' interests. The council is charged with creating a regional growth guide that provides a framework for land use, transit, wastewater, and the distribution of affordable housing across the region.[35] The council has its own taxing authority to raise revenue for its activities. This council embodies what john powell refers to as "federated regionalism," which is a "two-tier" form of metropolitan government, in which a regional governance council coordinates activity related to regional goals and interests (such as the siting of affordable housing or transit networks), while localities are given decision over matters that are local in nature.[36]

The Met Council had two notable early initiatives. One of the first focused on addressing the tax-base inequality that had emerged between jurisdictions in the Twin Cities region, in an effort to aid low-tax-wealth jurisdictions in the region. As noted in our description of Normandy in chapter 1, lower income communities (both cities and lower income suburbs) often struggle, due to historic patterns of discrimination, with low levels of investment and thus low levels of tax valuation, both in terms of commercial and residential property values. As a result, these communities have to tax themselves at a high rate to yield needed resources. These high tax rates—along with poor quality infrastructure and racial and economic segregation—leave these communities unable to compete with wealthier suburbs for commercial or industrial businesses, or for upper income residents. This creates a vicious cycle resulting in worsening disparities in tax bases between cities, low income suburbs, and affluent suburbs over time.[37]

In an attempt to address these disparities, the Minnesota state legislature enacted the nation's first tax-base sharing plan in the Twin Cities via the 1971 Fiscal Disparities Act, which sought to address economic inequity between cities and suburbs in the area by ensuring that any growth in commercial and industrial tax base was shared across the region, rather than enjoyed only by the wealthier suburbs, as is normally the case. As *Atlantic* writer Derek Thompson recently wrote in describing the origins of the plan:

> In the 1960s, local districts and towns in the Twin Cities region offered competing tax breaks to lure in new businesses, diminishing their revenues and depleting their social services in an effort to steal jobs from elsewhere within the area. In 1971, the region came up with an ingenious plan that would help halt this race to the bottom, and also address widening inequality. The Minnesota state legislature passed a law requiring all of the region's local governments—in Minneapolis and St. Paul and throughout their ring of suburbs—to contribute almost half of the growth in their commercial tax revenues to a regional pool, from which the money would be distributed to tax-poor areas. Today, business taxes are used to enrich some of the region's poorest communities.[38]

The Fiscal Disparities Act required each jurisdiction in the seven-county area to contribute to a regional pool 40 percent of the growth in the value of its commercial/industrial tax capacity. This narrowed the gap in tax revenue between high and low wealth communities in the region by 20 percent.[39] The tax-base sharing program gives cities some autonomy in setting their own tax rates, while still requiring them to contribute to a common pool.

The tax-base sharing meant that, instead of the zero-sum battle over tax resources between central cities and suburbs, the Twin Cities sought to ensure that the downtown area, inner-ring neighborhoods, and affluent suburbs all benefited from the economic success of the region. This resulted in an intentional "spreading the wealth" to all communities in the Twin Cities, including its poorest neighborhoods, rather than depriving cities and low wealth suburbs of resources as found in other sites in our Ford Foundation study such as Rochester, New York and Milwaukee.[40]

There are several reasons that tax-base sharing is preferable to state aid programs in reducing wealth disparities between cities and suburbs.[41] First, tax-base sharing can change the incentive of different localities to compete with each other; if the tax base is shared, there is less motivation for localities (cities and school systems) to use exclusionary tools to win the lion's share of business and/or affluent households. Second, tax-base sharing programs can be more sensitive to the needs of different districts across metropolitan regions, as opposed to a uniform state funding formula. Finally, tax-base sharing can also save the state money by redistributing revenue across a region, rather than requiring the infusion of additional state resources.[42]

While the Twin Cities' tax-base sharing plan is widely considered successful, the Met Council has been criticized as less effective than it could be, particularly around issues of equity. One key area of critique is that, because members of the council are appointed rather than elected, the council is not adequately accountable to the public.[43] Also, the Council has been critiqued for failing to exercise its authority over the key equity issues it was charged to address, particularly around fair housing.[44]

Several decades ago, fair housing had been a key early success in the region. Indeed, back at the time the tax-base sharing plan was instituted, the state of Minnesota was at the forefront of efforts to ensure affordable housing in all communities when it passed a law in 1976 requiring all local governments in the region to have their fair share of affordable housing. This resulted in the construction of low income housing in fast-growing suburbs and not just distressed areas of the central cities, as is common in many other metro areas. This meant that the city/suburban geography became less racialized in the Twin Cities, as compared to other areas, over this time period.[45]

The Twin Cities regional model thus had several key early successes. First, the tax-base sharing plan led to greater resource equity between jurisdictions across the region. Second, the housing plan led to a more balanced distribution of affordable housing across the region.[46] Indeed, the percentage of cities in the region offering affordable housing increased from 8 percent to 51 percent in the course of a decade.[47] The racial isolation of African Americans in the region also declined during this period.[48]

However, as Myron Orfield and Will Stancil write: "This commitment began to collapse in the mid-1980s. Political apathy about racial equality was accompanied by exclusionary housing practices in the suburbs."[49] Since that time, the region has abandoned its Metropolitan Council Housing Plan. This is in part, Orfield and Stancil argue, due to what they call the rise of the "poverty housing industry," which "centers around nonprofit housing developers but also includes funding intermediaries, for-profit tax credit syndicators, attorneys, and lobbyists."[50] Together these groups have worked to ensure that affordable housing is located primarily in segregated communities, rather than in integrated neighborhoods in the Minneapolis region.

Perhaps the most significant weakness of the regional effort in the Twin Cities is the failure of the Met Council to address the issue of educational inequality across the region. Indeed, schools have been largely unaddressed by the Met Council, despite the fact that the state legislation that initiated this regional structure states that the Met Council should focus on needs "including but not limited to such matters as land use, parks and open space land needs, the necessity for and location of airports, highways, transit facilities, public hospitals, libraries, *schools*, and other public buildings"[51] (emphasis added).

The problem of school segregation in the Twin Cities metro area is significant,[52] as the city of Minneapolis and inner-ring suburbs enroll ever-growing numbers of low income and minority students, while outlying suburban districts remain predominantly white and more affluent, as seen in figures 4.1 and 4.2. There have been efforts to address these problems, but these have occurred only through the courts and not through the Met Council. The main program targeting the problem

FIGURE 4.1

Minneapolis Metro: Percent Black and Latinx residents in school districts by census tract

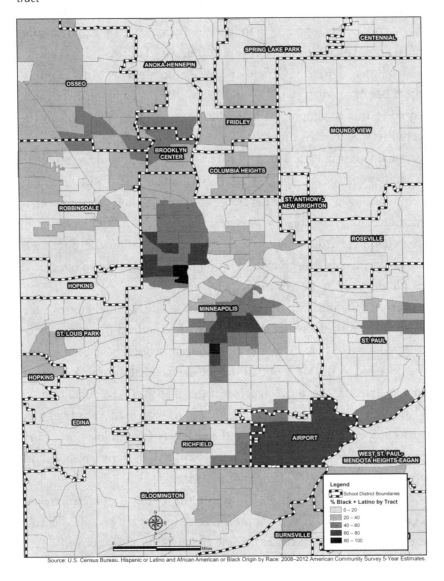

Source: U.S. Census Bureau. Hispanic or Latino and African American or Black Origin by Race: 2008–2012 American Community Survey 5-Year Estimates.

FIGURE 4.2

Minneapolis Metro: Percent of individuals under 18 years old in poverty in school districts by census tract

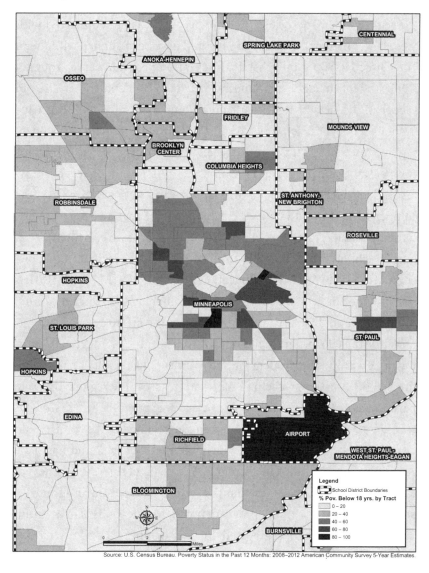

Source: U.S. Census Bureau. Poverty Status in the Past 12 Months: 2008–2012 American Community Survey 5-Year Estimates.

of segregation in the metro area is called the Choice is Yours (CIY), an interdistrict integration program, much like those described in chapter 3, that resulted from a court settlement in 2000.

We only briefly describe CIY here because it is not connected with these larger regional efforts, and yet could have been aligned with them. The Choice is Yours interdistrict integration program serves roughly 2,000 students in eight surrounding districts.[53] Students transferring to suburban districts bring the full aid amount associated with the Minneapolis School District, which is substantially more than the per-student rate for resident students in the receiving districts because of various compensatory aid programs in Minnesota.[54] As a result, for every transfer student out, Minneapolis district loses the state aid as well as the compensatory funds that go with the student.[55] Separate from the court settlement that created the CIY program, there are also two interdistrict magnet schools, which had been until 2015 run by the regional joint powers board called West Metro Education Program (WMEP).[56] WMEP has also provided professional development throughout the years on cultural proficiency and diversity for teachers across the metro area.

While the CIY program has offered some degree of integrated learning opportunities for students in the Minneapolis region, it has not addressed the broader problem of segregation across the region. This is in part because CIY has essentially been a one-way program, where students transfer out of Minneapolis, thus leaving segregation in the Minneapolis city schools largely untouched, much like the Rochester and East Palo Alto programs described in chapter 3. As a result of this, the Minneapolis district itself has been less than enthusiastic about the program. As someone affiliated with the program noted, Minneapolis is in a significant bind as an urban, segregated, low performing school district that is losing kids through multiple avenues—CIY as well as charter schools:

> My observation is that Minneapolis has stuff coming at them from all
> quarters, they're just a damn punching bag, political punching bag, and

some of it might be deserved, and most of it probably isn't . . . And it's a Catch-22, because if the kids in Choice Is Yours who go to the suburbs and do fabulously well, you would like to think that Minneapolis and everyone else would be saying, well, it's a good program, let's keep it going. The better those kids do, the worse it looks for Minneapolis, how do you win that one. And when the kids . . . if they don't do better, people say, well, you need to fold it up, they're not doing better.

Had a stronger Met Council intervened to require that suburbs continue to accept students, ensuring a stronger two-way program that benefited Minneapolis, or been more assertive in ensuring a regional distribution of affordable housing across the region's suburbs, it might have helped to address the ongoing segregation in the Minneapolis–St. Paul region.

The problem of school segregation was also left unaddressed by another strong regional government, in Portland, Oregon. Portland's model is widely considered successful in that it is credited with preventing the hollowing out of the urban core, which has been common in many metro areas. In 1978, voters agreed to establish the Metropolitan Service District (MSD), to address growing problems related to regional fragmentation,[57] and a Metro Council, charged with establishing the regional growth boundary in the area, limiting fringe development and sprawl. The Metro Council, whose members are elected (rather than appointed, like the Twin Cities' Met Council) was granted operational responsibilities over waste disposal, public transit, and the zoo.[58]

Portland's Metro government has been considered largely successful on many fronts. According to regionalism scholars Peter Drier, John Mollenkopf, and Todd Swanstrom, "Portland Metro largely achieved its goals for coordinating land use planning and transportation policy, extending public transit, revitalizing older neighborhoods, and strengthening the downtown business district."[59] Further, the adoption of the Metropolitan Housing Rule by the Oregon state legislature in 1995, "which requires the twenty-seven jurisdictions in the region to accommodate their fair share of affordable housing by reducing minimum lot size requirements,"[60] has been credited with the relatively lower rates of economic segregation in the region.[61]

Yet the Portland Metro has been criticized for some key weaknesses. For example, it does not administer housing programs, and as a result, affordable housing programs are not coordinated across the region.[62] Most significantly, it has not had any policy authority over the school systems in the region.

Thus, the Twin Cities and Portland areas have—at least to some degree—emerged as noteworthy examples of places that have developed policies and practices that alter the power structures in metropolitan areas so that racialized spaces are not deprived of political and economic resources. However, policymakers in these two metros have also unfortunately allowed localism to thrive in decisions that have been made (or not made) around the public education system, as well as in housing, in ways that undercut the overarching goals relating to regional equity.

THE NEED FOR A BIGGER, BOLDER APPROACH

The case studies presented here suggest that regional solutions are an important policy tool that have been promoted by urban policymakers and planners. To address the problems of segregation and resource inequality, as well as the underlying dynamic of competition between cities and suburbs that drives regional inequities, regional policy solutions must have a strong, common vision among a diverse group of stakeholders as well as strong alignment across sectors. Finally, regional solutions like the ones discussed in the Twin Cities and Portland metro areas are not sufficient unless they integrate education with other social policy issues. Without incorporating educational inequities into these broader issues, segregation and the issues that result from concentrated poverty in urban communities will continue and will enable suburban communities to thrive at the expense of their central cities.

The urban regional solutions presented in this chapter have isolated education from the other urban policy areas. This is likely due to the high political stakes involved and the vested interests in many parties in the status quo. But avoiding education in regional solutions ultimately leaves a key driver of regional inequality unaddressed. At the same time, tackling educational issues without also tackling some of the underlying drivers of educational inequity, such as housing, transit, and workforce or economic development, is insufficient, and will have weak results given the political dynamics we have discussed previously. Even in the best case examples of efforts to target educational inequity through specific policy strategies—like the ones discussed in chapters 2 and 3—commitment to equity usually diminishes over time as a result of both politics and other policy pressures. In the next chapter, we lay out an agenda for a bigger, bolder approach that involves comprehensive reform around regional equity.

FIVE

A Regional Policy Framework
for Addressing Inequality

IN THE EARLY 2000S, the Omaha Public Schools were facing serious difficulties. Over the three prior decades, the district had lost thousands of white and middle-class families to suburban schools, as well as the tax dollars that went with them. The district's tax base was further depleted by redevelopment deals struck by the city that gave tax breaks to corporations to lure them to relocate into the city center. As one participant in our study noted, the downtown redevelopment meant good things for the city's finances, but did not help the school system's tax base: "You drive back past Con Agra, you see all the fancy buildings coming in, it's fine, they're tax-exempted. No one has said, 'How's that impacting the tax base and the property revenue that you're able to generate for the services to kids?' I consider that silence neglect."

Strapped for resources, the district leadership appealed to the state legislature for more funding, but according to our interviews, their calls were met with silence. As a result, the district filed a school finance lawsuit against the state, hoping for relief in the courts but knowing that the fight would be long and difficult. Then, in 2004, an unusual policy development related to the expansion rights of the Omaha school district gave the Omaha district leaders some hope.

Understanding this policy development requires understanding the history of the Omaha district's expansion rights. Throughout the early twentieth century, the Omaha school district had the right to expand its territory whenever the city annexed outlying territory. As one participant in our study recalled:

> As the city of Omaha grew, so grew the Omaha Public Schools. As the city annexed south Omaha, the school—now South High School—became part of the Omaha Public Schools. As the city of Omaha annexed Benson, Benson community became part of the Omaha Public School community . . . [and] in 1969 the city of Omaha annexed Irvington, and sure enough, the Irvington Public Schools became part of the Omaha Public Schools the following year . . . Up until the 1970s, as the city of Omaha grew, so grew the Omaha Public Schools.

But starting in the 1970s, the school district stopped expanding alongside the city, with no official record as to why this practice had ended. Some speculate that it was due to a behind-the-scenes agreement to protect suburbs from the threat of court-ordered school desegregation in Omaha. As one city leader noted: "I find it interesting . . . at the very time that the integration movement in the Omaha Public Schools [was] going on, you find the [school board] records silent with respect to any conversation about [annexation] at all."

The end result was that the city continued to annex surrounding communities, leading it to grow in size and in tax base, but the school district was frozen—and, in fact, shrinking in enrollment and in the number of middle-class students as these students moved over the district boundaries into the surrounding suburban districts or used the state's school choice laws to flee to suburban schools. As one observer noted, the families who left gained advantages for their children simply by moving into a different district: "All that happened is students stepped over a line, and families simply experienced the opportunities that come with a significant difference in funding level."

By the early 2000s, the ability of the school district to expand seemed all but forgotten by most in this community. According to our interviews, the issue re-emerged in late 2004, when the school district's lawyers were reviewing a bill; while reading the fine print, they discovered that it eliminated the district's annexation powers. This effort to eliminate the district's annexation powers was occurring right when the city of Omaha had initiated annexation proceedings against another suburb, suggesting to some of the people we interviewed that this was not coincidental.[1]

The leadership of the Omaha school district was furious at this behind-the-scenes maneuver, particularly since the legislature had denied giving it more resources. On June 6, 2005, before the law could pass, the school board made a bold move: it voted to utilize the long-forgotten state law and annex *all* of the territory within the Omaha city limits. The board unanimously passed a resolution to "take all necessary steps to assure that all schools organized or existing within the city of Omaha are under the direction of OPS." This meant that the Omaha school district would annex twenty-five schools in two suburban districts, Elkhorn and Millard. Their effort to bring all schools located within the Omaha city limits under the purview of the Omaha Public Schools was called One City, One School District.

Suburban school systems were taken off guard by this move. As a former superintendent of one suburban district recalled: "I came home after a board meeting night, so it was a Monday night, and I think it's like June 6, 2005, and I'm just sort of listening to the news at ten, and my wife says, 'Did you hear that?' And I go, 'Hear what?' And she says, 'Well, Omaha just announced a One City, One School District policy.'

Which in effect, takes over a good chunk of the Millard schools and a good chunk of the Elkhorn schools."

The outcry by the suburbs was immediate and intense. A number of public meetings were held, many filled with angry suburban parents. The Omaha superintendent received numerous death threats. After a great deal of political debate, the legislature became the focus for a solution. Through negotiation, they worked out a compromise in the form of a law that restored the former suburban district boundaries to their prior state, thus returning the twenty-five schools back to the suburban districts. In exchange, the law established the Learning Community of Douglas and Sarpy Counties, which was designed to address some of the key complaints of the Omaha school board.[2]

As compared with the narrower interdistrict integration plans discussed in chapter 3, the Learning Community solution is unique in that it is a *regional* educational solution, requiring cooperation across all eleven districts in the metro area to address the problems faced by OPS and its families. The Learning Community involves four key elements: a tax-base-sharing plan, an interdistrict integration plan to address the segregation in the region (see figures 5.1 and 5.2), a redistributive tax, and a regional governing council. These are discussed more fully in the later sections of this chapter.

The regional nature of the Learning Community policy stands in stark contrast to recent educational policies, which, as we discussed in chapter 2, tend to leave city school districts on their own to solve or deal with their problems (i.e., racial segregation, poverty concentration, and school funding problems), and which often prescribe narrow or punitive approaches that do not attack the bigger challenges of poverty and segregation. Importantly, the Learning Community also entails *educational* regional policy—which is lacking from the other regional approaches we described in chapter 4. As noted earlier, in many regional policy discussions, educational inequality constitutes a key part of the diagnosis of the problem; yet, the movements for regional equity have focused largely on noneducational reforms in municipal governance, transit, and the environment; educational policy has been left off the table.

The Learning Community model has been somewhat modified since its inception, but the model, at least in its original design, offers a promising example upon which to build a broader regional movement to address not only educational equity but many of the core issues of concern to those in the regionalism world (housing segregation, tax-base inequality, transit, land use, etc.). The Learning Community embodies the federated regionalism approach discussed previously, in that it is governed by an elected metropolitan board known as the Learning Community Coordinating Council; at the same time, individual school boards retain control over key decisions of curriculum, budgeting, staffing, and other areas.[3] As previously discussed, federated regionalism is a two-tier form of metropolitan government, in which a regional governance council coordinates activity related to regional goals and interests (i.e., the siting of affordable housing or transit networks), while localities are given decision-making authority over matters that are local in nature.[4] Federated regionalism, as civil rights professor and lawyer john powell notes, is "based on two premises: first, many important problems within the inner cities and older suburbs can only be dealt with adequately at a regional level; and second, some issues, or some aspects of issues, are of a local nature and thus are more effectively handled by a local government."[5]

The federated regional approach is an approach that addresses regional inequality but is less drastic than proposals to *consolidate* jurisdictions—that is, to merge city and suburban governments, or merge city and suburban school systems.[6] This type of consolidation has happened in a handful of metro areas in the past several decades, and is what was proposed by the Ferguson Commission report in the St. Louis metro area, which attributed racial tensions between the police and the community in the St. Louis area to a fragmented system of government that reduced

FIGURE 5.1

Omaha Metro: Percent Black and Latinx residents in school districts by census tract

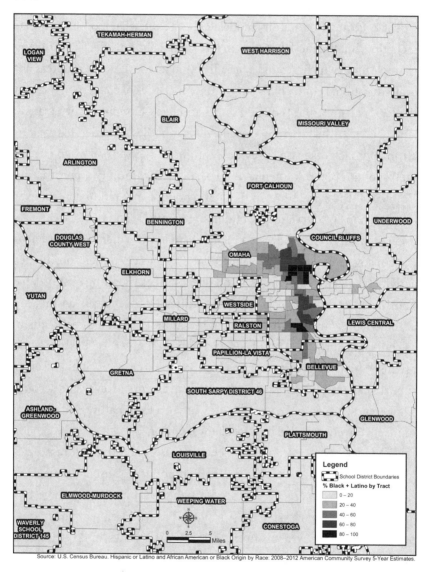

Source: U.S. Census Bureau. Hispanic or Latino and African American or Black Origin by Race: 2008–2012 American Community Survey 5-Year Estimates.

FIGURE 5.2

Omaha Metro: Percent of individuals under 18 years old in poverty in school districts by census tract

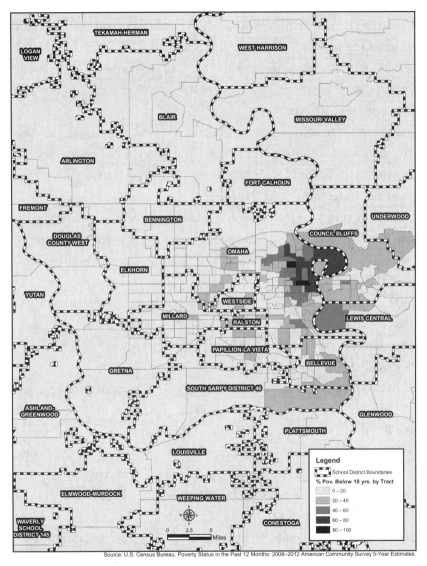

Source: U.S. Census Bureau. Poverty Status in the Past 12 Months: 2008–2012 American Community Survey 5-Year Estimates.

tax resources in low income communities, causing police departments to increase local fees to increase revenues, resulting in increased traffic stops and leading to increased police-community conflict. As we mentioned in earlier chapters, while consolidation has been viewed as successful in attacking regional inequities, it is politically difficult to accomplish due to suburban resistance, and also because communities of color with long-standing identities, culture, and history are not keen to see their communities dissolved.[7]

In contrast to consolidation, a federated regional system can address difficult issues of housing and school segregation and resource inequality, while still allowing local communities with long histories and strong identities to remain intact. However, it must be designed carefully in order to ensure a central and sustained focus on equity. Indeed, as we noted in chapter 4, the few federated regional arrangements that do exist lean toward less controversial issues—at least on face value—like transportation and wastewater, and turn away from thornier problems like segregation and resource distribution. To truly move forward on these entrenched issues around regional inequities across multiple sectors, a community must develop the political will to tackle these difficult issues, as we will discuss in detail in chapter 6.

In this chapter, we lay out our vision for the federated regional equity approach to address the core problems discussed in this book. We use Omaha as the example throughout this chapter, as this metro area implemented a number of key elements that we believe are important to regional equity and, unlike any other community across the country, Omaha centered its focus on educational equity. Through the story of Omaha and the Learning Community reform, we describe the five core pillars of a regional equity framework: tax-base sharing, place-based policies, mobility policies, regional governance, and cross-sector approaches. Many of these ideas are not new, and some have been proposed in the urban policy world, yet nowhere have they been implemented in combination. In addition, we offer here a regional educational equity lens, which has rarely been incorporated.

FEDERATED REGIONALISM IN OMAHA: A FOUNDATION FOR A BROADER MOVEMENT

Our core argument has been that many of the inequities entrenched in the US educational system are caused by broader dynamics across a region—particularly the systems of competitive relationships between school districts that, when overlaid on historic patterns of housing and school segregation and economic development, contribute to deepening inequality and segregation. Change thus requires dismantling both these systems of relationships and the inequities upon which they are based.

Below, we describe the core elements of our federated regional equity approach, drawing from Omaha's Learning Community as an exemplar of these approaches. We highlight the importance of each element in developing the broader regional strategy that we argue for. While some of the elements of the Learning Community have recently been dismantled due to political resistance (as we discuss at the end of the chapter), in this discussion we focus on the core elements of the Learning Community as originally designed, because they stand as exemplars of the multi-pronged policy that we think is most fruitful.

Strategy 1: Tax-Base Sharing and Resource Redistribution

One key problem created by fragmented local governments is fiscal inequality, with some localities clear winners, while others struggle to stay afloat. This was apparent in the Normandy story we described in chapter 1, where the Normandy district, consisting of twenty-four local small communities, had to tax themselves at a very high rate to yield needed resources to fund their schools—and even those resources weren't enough.

Thus, one key goal of regional equity efforts must be to address the fiscal inequality and the system of relationships—particularly the competitive relationships between cities and suburbs (and between different types of suburbs) that drive such inequality. While many state aid programs, including state school-finance equalization schemes, provide money to localities to compensate for low tax bases, these programs often fail to fully address the inequities and are politically vulnerable—often subject to cuts in lean economic times, creating further inequities.

Tax-base sharing, as outlined in chapter 4, on the other hand, involves pooling and then redistributing taxes across a metro area. It is based on the premise that all residents in a metro area should benefit from regional growth, rather than just a select and elite few. Tax-base sharing involves the contribution of a portion of a jurisdiction's local revenue to a regional pool, which is then redistributed based on locally decided criteria, such as equalization. As we noted in chapter 4, tax-base sharing has been attempted in a handful of metropolitan areas to date, including the Twin Cities, where municipalities contribute 40 percent of the growth in the value of commercial-industrial tax capacity to a regional pool that then gets redistributed based on local population and to compensate cities with lower-than-average values.

The Learning Community's tax-base sharing plan has been one of the few created on a metropolitan level in education policy. As originally designed, the Learning Community's plan pooled all local tax resources designated for education for the purpose of creating school funding equity across a region. According to a former Nebraska state senator who helped to draft the original Learning Community legislation:

> You need a common financial base . . . You can't have a deal where . . . we can use our, perhaps, very strong valuation base to make sure that my kids, even though not at-risk kids, get educated very well, and your kids, you know, are . . . oh, gosh, that's too bad, but that's all you've got, and you're gonna have to make do with that. So, you know, if we all have to make do with less, then we all have to make do with less. We don't just say, well, ok, it's the at-risk kids that deal with less and the, you know,

kids from the higher income families are fine. So, you needed a common financial base.[8]

Under the original Learning Community plan, the tax bases of all eleven school districts were merged, and then taxed using a base uniform tax rate. Funds were then redistributed to local districts based upon the state funding formula that takes into account student need. In each case, localities maintained decision-making power over their own tax rates, and could opt to tax themselves at a higher rate than the regional rate to yield additional revenue.

As one Learning Community administrator noted, the sharing of tax resources via the common levy across the metro area was appropriate, because families in high wealth suburban districts should contribute some of their wealthy tax base to lower income districts like the Omaha public schools, since those families benefit from the institutions (e.g., arts, library, etc.) and infrastructure (highways, etc.) that have been built in those low wealth districts. This administrator remarked:

> I think the common levy exists to create an equitable playing field so that adequate resources exist for all 197 buildings [in the metro area], to responsibly educate the children that they have. And I believe in the common levy because [a high performing suburban school system] could not be as robust and productive and healthy economically as it is if it didn't feed off a larger city. I mean, that's just reality. So, if we are economically interdependent on each other for the health and well-being of those various boundaries that we love so much, aren't we equally impacted if we have literally a whole generation of students who are not succeeding in school? . . . So that's why I feel common levy is legitimate because if you're crossing over your boundaries for work and pleasure, and all that, economically, how can then you draw these finite boundaries for educational dollars and say, well, that's your lot in life, that's what your boundaries look like, so that's all the money you should get to use. So, you know . . . so, that's the resource, that's the financial resource factor to help the achievement gap.

Although the common levy was phased out in 2016, analyses did show that the Learning Community's tax-base sharing system had worked as intended: the districts with the lowest tax wealth and high proportions of low income students received the most aid under the system (although for a number of reasons, particularly the phase-in timeline, these gains were not immediately realized.)[9] Furthermore, reports found that the state saved money because the redistribution among districts lowered the amount of state aid required.[10]

There are a number of benefits to metropolitan regional tax-base sharing programs when compared to the state aid programs that exist in many states. First, such programs can be more cost-effective than state aid programs for reducing disparities among school districts or municipalities; when local revenue is redistributed amongst localities in a region, it saves the state significant costs in equalization aid required by the state, as occurred in Omaha.[11] In other words, when taxes are shared across regions, less contribution is required by taxpayers in other parts of the state.

Second, and most significantly, tax-base sharing changes the underlying dynamics of the system, by reducing the incentives for high wealth municipalities to engage in actions that enhance their advantages—such as luring corporations through tax breaks (which harms both the locality and others) and relying on exclusionary zoning (such as prohibiting multifamily or affordable housing). In other words, with tax-base sharing, high wealth municipalities can't yield as much revenue from exclusionary practices. In this way, tax-base sharing not only equalizes resources across a region, it also has the potential to change the rules of the game by reducing the incentives for competition between localities, thereby creating more equity between municipalities and school systems.

But municipal and educational tax-base sharing should not be kept separate—they should be accompanied by complementary strategies across the region for economic development. As in the Twin Cities, strategies don't have to involve full tax-base sharing—they can, for example, only entail the growth in tax resources from one year to the next, or a portion thereof. Regardless, connecting the fate of communities in terms of tax resources—given that they are already connected economically—is a critical element in altering the competitive dynamics that undermine equity between localities and between school systems.

Strategy 2: In-Place Investment Policies Funded by Regional Resources

The second regional equity strategy that we advocate for is what john powell calls "in-place" strategies: policies that are focused on directing investment and resources into high poverty and traditionally marginalized communities. These are aimed at ensuring that communities that have been historically deprived of investment due to the regional dynamics we have laid out in this book receive resources and support.

The Learning Community involves one such in-place *educational* strategy, which is the establishment of "elementary learning centers," community centers that provide social and academic support services to children and parents outside of school hours (e.g., parental reading skills, English classes for families, or health centers).[12] The learning centers are funded through a small regional tax levied across all eleven districts, and thus are supported by a small contribution from everyone across the metro area. By law, these centers are located in the highest poverty neighborhoods in the Learning Community, both of which are within the Omaha school district boundaries. As a state official notes of the centers:

> Elementary learning centers are not schools; they are institutions to support the work of schools, and they are to be created with certain criteria in the areas of greatest need, and that was primarily the Omaha Public Schools . . . and so they're to be places of healthcare, places of extended learning, before and after school, places to match parents and kids up with services that they needed to support their learning in elementary school.

Over time, some of the funding for the elementary learning centers was shifted to allow other districts beyond Omaha to have access to the funds. Those funds were used for such programs as kindergarten readiness, extended learning time (before- and afterschool tutoring) and summer learning programs. Spreading the resources to more school districts was seen as a way to increase political buy-in. Over 10,000 students were served by learning center programming in 2013/14, and evaluation results were positive in terms of both child and family outcomes.[13]

The type of in-place or place-based strategies utilized by the Learning Community are not new. In education, such strategies have long been exemplified in the community schools movement, which is a reform movement aimed at transforming traditional public schools into community hubs that offer wraparound health and social services, as well as afterschool and summer programming.[14] Many K–12 community schools also involve adult education or adult services. As education professors Terrance Green and Mark Gooden write, "community schools aim to build neighborhood-wide social capital and position productive partnerships as an integral component to school and neighborhood improvements."[15] Community schools are therefore intended to address educational inequity and also serve as a tool for broader neighborhood investment and development.[16]

In-place strategies have also been a focus of urban federal policy, embodied primarily in community development approaches.[17] During the War on Poverty in the 1960s, the federal government supported the creation of Community Development Corporations (CDCs), whose goals are to coordinate both federal grants and local investment to improve distressed neighborhoods. Current estimates indicate that approximately 3,600 CDCs are currently in operation.[18] Manuel Pastor and his colleagues note that CDCs focus on "building and rebuilding housing, launching commercial developments, and running various programs in areas as diverse as job trainings and parent education."[19] Typically, the boards of CDCs consist of community members, with at least one-third of the board comprised of community residents, "allowing for the possibility of direct, grassroots participation in decision making."[20]

Some research has shown positive outcomes of CDCs. Wayne State professor George Galster and colleagues conducted a mixed-method analysis of five CDC communities and found that in all of these communities the CDCs played an important role in in helping neighborhoods improve.[21] Yet critics of the community development approach argue that the strategy has not lived up to its promise of significant, long-term improvement in distressed communities. Urban scholar David Rusk argues, for example, that despite the commitment and hard work of these agencies, they are limited in their potential given the underlying regional dynamics that consistently work against the communities that CDCs seek to bolster. He writes that, "In effect, CDCs are expected to help a crowd of poor people run up a down escalator, an escalator that is engineered to come down faster than most poor people can run up."[22] Rusk argues that the CDC paradigm, by focusing on the (re)development of isolated communities, does not tackle the underlying causes of that isolation; in this way, the paradigm "allows powerful institutions to shirk once again their responsibility to confront racial and economic segregation."[23]

In a similar analogy, Pastor and his colleagues note that community development advocacy groups often are swimming upstream against powerful forces. "The gap between promise and performance arises in part because CDC activities are the equivalent of swimming against a raging stream—one in which the challenge is not water but a phalanx of policies and contexts that discourage investment in poor inner-city neighborhoods, and encourage outward sprawl to suburbs and exurbs."[24]

One of the limits (or at the very least, challenges) of in-place strategies such as community schools and community development is sustainability. Both community development and community schools often rely on local benefactors, foundations, or government grants for support; such sources of funds are often short-term, and not always self-sustaining.

While in-place approaches are highly worthy of pursuit, our work suggests that these will have limited impact and sustainability unless incorporated within a broader regional framework that attacks the structures of inequality themselves. Thus, in-place approaches must be accompanied by broader regional equity strategies, such as revenue sharing or the regional tax that we noted supported the elementary learning centers in Omaha—a regional tax which cost the average resident very little (less than $23/year for an owner of a $150,000 home),[25] but which yielded significant and sustainable revenue for the centers. Such regional resources make in-place strategies sustainable over the long term.

Strategy 3: Mobility Policies

The third component of the regional equity framework we propose is usually referred to as "mobility strategies," strategies that seek to improve opportunities by moving people across boundary lines and "toward opportunity."[26] Mobility strategies seek to break down patterns of racial and economic segregation in both housing and schools.

In education, an example of a mobility strategy is the interdistrict integration programs we have described in previous chapters that seek to help lower income students and students of color cross district boundary lines and access improved educational opportunities. The Learning Community also provides an exemplar of a similar educational mobility strategy: it incorporated an interdistrict integration program designed to increase socioeconomic integration across all schools in the Omaha metro area. The program as originally designed (though revised in 2016) encouraged students to transfer between schools in different districts, with priority and transportation given to students who enhance the socioeconomic balance of a school building. The ultimate goal of the program was to ensure that each school in all eleven metro-area school districts had the same proportion of low income students as the metro-wide average. As one of the legislators who helped craft the legislation noted, the interdistrict integration plan was not just about reducing the concentration of poverty; it also enabled districts to take advantage of the diversity across school districts in the metro area: "The idea is that your educational opportunity is enhanced by having the opportunity to go to class with a diverse group of students . . . you know, the idea is to take advantage of the diversity, the population diversity, rather than to partition it off."[27]

The program was popular, and by the last year of the program, approximately 2,800 students were engaging in school transfers that increased the socioeconomic diversity of the receiving school.[28] But the program structure was altered in 2016 by the legislature: starting in 2017, the state no longer pays for free transit for any student who increases the SES diversity of a school building, and now only funds transit for those eligible for free lunch, thus significantly reducing the incentive for transfers by higher income students into lower income schools.[29]

The Learning Community model also included interdistrict magnets or "focus schools," which were designed to attract and enroll students from across all eleven districts in the metro area. The legislation incentivized the creation of those schools by providing a per-pupil funding incentive and capital funds that, with the approval of the coordinating council, would allow a district that wanted to build a focus school to get part of the funding to construct the school, thus providing a regionally sustainable source of funding. The Learning Community has since approved three focus programs, all within Omaha Public Schools: Wilson Focus School (serving grades 2–5), as well as focus programs within two schools: Lewis and Clark Middle School and Burke High School. In 2016, the regional funding for this program was cut with the elimination of the common levy, forcing these schools to continue to operate via Omaha school district funding.

Each of these programs in the Learning Community utilized school choice policies to promote diversity across school buildings. Yet it is critically important to acknowledge that integration and diversity don't automatically translate into improved cross-racial understanding or improved opportunities for traditionally marginalized students. There are many examples of ways in which racially diverse schools work to marginalize students of color academically and socially, through unequal access to advanced coursework, through differential treatment in discipline, through marginalizing curriculum, and through microaggressions by teachers and students.[30] If implemented, schools and districts must directly tackle these dynamics.

While school choice policies to promote integration are an important component of a regional equity strategy, one of the most fundamental ways to break down inequality and segregation between school districts is by changing the geographic distribution of affordable housing—specifically by building more housing, or providing access to housing, in high opportunity neighborhoods, near better performing, low poverty schools.[31] Currently, however, federal affordable housing dollars often reinforce, rather than reduce, segregation. This is true of several of the government's largest affordable housing programs: the Housing Choice Voucher (HCV) program, formerly known as Section 8, which provides low income families with rental assistance on the private market; Project-Based Section 8, where the government contracts directly with landlords who then make units available for low income households;[32] and the Low Income Housing Tax Credit Program, which served 13 million householders as of 2013.[33]

Housing policy should not only address the deficiencies of these programs—in terms of the barriers they pose to allowing low income families access to housing in high opportunity neighborhoods—but they should specifically prioritize housing built near high opportunity schools. As Virginia Commonwealth University education professor Genevieve Siegel-Hawley writes, such a move would "represent a marked departure of the segregating ways these low income housing subsidies have traditionally been disbursed."[34]

One solution to this problem was developed in Chicago, where a regional housing program, called the Regional Housing Initiative (RHI) was created. This regional housing initiative was overseen by the area's Metropolitan Planning Organization. The goal was to increase the supply of affordable housing in high opportunity areas. Schools were a key part of the equation: the "RHI developed an opportunity index that weighted equally indicators of poverty, housing stability, job access, labor market engagement, school performance, and transit access." The index uses rates of reading and math proficiency on state exams.[35] A summary report on the initiative's progress notes:

> RHI was built by a broad set of engaged stakeholders who recognized the value of the Housing Choice Voucher program as a tool for supporting a range of housing options in areas characterized by good schools, jobs, and transit. Despite barriers such as community resistance to affordable housing and negative perceptions of the HCV program and the families it serves, RHI and its stakeholders implemented a workable operating model that aligns public housing resources with local and regional priorities.

Another example of a housing integration solution that incorporates schools is from Texas, where reforms occurred with the location of affordable housing that was funded by the Low Income Housing Tax Credit Program. A lawsuit charged that the state had been awarding its federally allocated tax credits in a way that fueled segregation. In response, the state changed the point system it used for deciding which developments were awarded the housing tax credits. Extra points were awarded to proposed developments located in low poverty neighborhoods and near high performing schools, thus increasing their chances of getting the credits. After the changes took effect in 2013, there was a significant increase in the number of multifamily developments that were built in low poverty neighborhoods in Texas, according to a report by the Texas Low Income Housing Information Service.[36]

These strategies must be accompanied by educational policy shifts— for example, where housing is developed in higher income white areas, supports should be provided for students of color because of the racial prejudices and structural racism they will likely encounter; training should be provided to teachers to ensure that they are prepared to teach diverse populations with culturally relevant materials and approaches; and steps should be taken to ensure that access to advanced courses is equitable. It is also important that student assignment policies are adjusted so schools do not become re-segregated, whether through school choice or through the manipulation of attendance zones. As students of color or poor students move to more white and affluent communities, historically these have been the responses that result.[37]

Strategy 4: Regional Governance

The three strategies described above form what one of our interviewees in Omaha called "three legs of a stool." Continuing this analogy, the "seat" of the stool—the fourth regional equity strategy we propose—is oversight of implementation through a regional governing body consisting of elected representatives from across the entire region. This should ensure a diverse group of stakeholders who are invested in developing a collective vision and ensuring continued focus on regional equity.

As mentioned in chapter 4, there are currently two regional decision-making bodies in the US that are explicitly focused on equity-minded regional development and vested with significant powers to achieve regional goals: Portland's Metro Council, serving twenty-four cities across three counties with a seven-member board (six of whom are elected, one is appointed), oversees twenty-one operational responsibilities (e.g., providing waste disposal and operating the zoo), and also holds policy-making authority (e.g., transportation and fair-share housing); and Minneapolis–St. Paul's Met Council, consisting of seventeen governor-appointed members that set policy guidelines for land use, housing, sewage, and parks.[38]

In addition, the Learning Community in Omaha has the sole elected regional governing body dedicated to educational policy issues across a metro area, the Learning Community Coordinating Council (LCCC). The LCCC oversees the tax-base sharing plan and the regional SES-based integration plan discussed above. It is a two-tier federated regionalist governing structure, in that the governing council oversees regional equity goals, while giving local school boards autonomy over other key decisions.

The LCCC's twenty-one members are elected from six equal-proportion voting districts across the entire metropolitan area. Twelve members are elected via "limited voting" from six geographic subdistricts, each of which elects two representatives each. The voting process is designed to increase the representation of minorities by allowing an unlimited number of people to run for election within a subdistrict. The top two vote-getters within each subdistrict win. This voting strategy, in theory, enables members of particular interest groups to cluster their votes around a particular candidate.[39] Such voting strategies, along with the federated regionalist governing structure, powell notes, can ensure that traditionally marginalized communities have a political voice no matter where they live:

> [It] gives minorities the choice to stay in their communities and strive for more equitable regional plans that will improve their neighborhoods (as well as the entire region) or move from their communities and retain their political power through their pooling of interests. In-place and mobility strategies become more a matter of personal choice, because no matter where minorities live, they can remain politically cohesive.[40]

Within a regional governing body, it is critical to not only have representation of all groups, but also to have a representation from the various political communities that are in the region. Thus, in Omaha, the voting structure was also designed to ensure representation across all school districts, even those not represented through direct elections. In addition to the twelve directly elected members from each of the six subdistricts (who consist of local citizens who run for the board), an additional six members are appointed by a caucus of local school board members (one from each subdistrict) in order to ensure that locally elected school board members are represented on the council. The final three members, who are non-voting, are appointed by school boards who fail to win representation in the other processes; these individuals can be either local citizens or school board members (but not school administrators) of their respective districts.

A former state senator, who was one of the crafters of the Learning Community legislation, noted the Learning Community governance structure is unique in involving both competition and cooperation:

> You still have individual school boards, each district is governed individually, but they all become a part of the Learning Community, which has a governance . . . The idea is that school districts still have a competitive relationship, you want to, in fact, foster that, you want school districts to compete with each other in providing the best opportunities for students and thereby attracting the students, and so on, but you also want them to cooperate with each other in the sense of, these students that live in east Omaha, or wherever they happen to live, are, in fact, students that we're all responsible for, so we all need to have programs to serve those students.[41]

Regional decision-making bodies like the LCCC are necessary to coordinate decisions on a regional scale and ensure commitment to equity projects in localities that may be resistant—for example, the siting of affordable housing (as in Minneapolis and Chicago); or regional educational policy decisions (such as integration programs, magnet schools, or community schools.). Further, based on our research on the Learning Community and regional governance in the Twin Cities and Portland, a regional body must be given authority to make decisions on key equity issues and be able to enforce compliance; without pressure, affluent localities are unlikely to accept affordable housing or agree to a school integration program, for example.[42] A regional body can also be the provider or coordinator of educational services, such as professional development around school diversity, for example.

Strategy 5: Cross-Sector Approaches

The final strategy we argue for within our framework is the use of cross-sector approaches, where educational policy is not pursued in isolation from other strategies but in tandem with housing, transit, health, economic development, etc. Such cross-sector approaches (more than mere coordination) can and should be pursued with respect to all the strategies above.

There are a number of natural cross-sector connections to be made within place-based strategies. For example, education can be (and in many places already is) linked to community development: many CDCs have incorporated education as part of their community development strategies (such as through child and adult literacy programs),[43] but these linkages can be made more systematic and broad-based, and can be better aligned with traditional public school systems. Further, community schools are a natural fit with community development, and thus should partner with CDCs as much as possible to leverage the power of both movements for positive neighborhood change in housing, education, and employment. Community schools can form a natural hub for the kind of neighborhood organizing that CDCs often seek to accomplish.[44]

Cross-sector connections can also occur with respect to mobility-based strategies. One example is with housing policy, which can be (and in some cases is being) oriented around educational access—that is, through the construction of affordable housing near low poverty schools, which we noted previously has already occurred in a number of locales, including Texas and Chicago.

There are also examples of coordination across other domains, such as transit and employment, and we argue that education must be integrated into such strategies. For example, the Jobs Access and Reverse Commute program, created in 1998, was a program designed to help low income individuals and welfare recipients access employment—specifically low-wage, low-education, entry-level positions, which are often located far from where such individuals reside. The program was repealed in 2012 and consolidated into other funding streams. A similar program could, in theory, be revived and coordinated with education. This was done in the Learning Community at the behest of a state senator who helped to advocate for having the interdistrict integration plan within the Learning Community. Due to this senator's advocacy, the law incorporated a transportation provision that low income parents (those whose children were eligible for free lunches) would be eligible for reimbursement for mileage, using the state mileage reimbursement rate, to transport their children to schools that they chose through the program. According to the senator, who had previously worked in public housing, this provision was important because it would help parents access jobs that were not available where they lived:

> One of the reasons that the open enrollment was important to me was really employment of parents, you know, so many parents, moms mostly, that I am familiar with working in public housing . . . The jobs aren't there, the jobs aren't where they live, so the idea of open enrollment, to me, [is] also about job opportunity, where if the mom got a job out here [in the suburbs], let's say, or Paypal, or one of the large companies that would hire someone with maybe just a high school education or a GED, that they could take their children to a school in the area of the business, so . . . and their transportation would be paid for because they're transporting their child to school.

Lastly, cross-sector coordination can occur around the third strategy, governance—where educational decisions are not made in isolation from housing and transit and economic development decisions, but in conjunction with them on the regional level. As we noted previously, regional governing structures already exist in most metro areas in the form of Metropolitan Planning Organizations, but their discussions almost never involve educational equity. As noted in chapter 4, they tend to be weak in their current form, but they could be strengthened and should incorporate education. A regional governance structure, some argue, adds an unnecessary layer of government, yet as a state senator we interviewed says below, this is needed to address the broader costs of the inequitable and inefficient system that does exist:

> Though you're gonna get political arguments, you're creating another level of government, but you're actually, by doing . . . by creating this layer of government, you're actually addressing a costly system of failure, a failing system is costly. So even if you're adding a little bit of extra government and it may be costly to do that, you're saving all sorts of social costs, and other costs involving in failing students.[45]

This layer of government becomes critical to maintaining and sustaining a focus on regional equity, and building upon structures that already exist would be politically wise given the pushback around extra layers of government.

OVERCOMING POLITICAL CHALLENGES

These five policy elements form the basis for a comprehensive educational policy approach that goes from a narrow, single-district, blame-the-schools focus, to a broader attack on the systems and structures that create failure in the first place. The core question remains: How does a community accomplish this, and how do they overcome the political geography and localism that have undermined so many efforts?

Indeed, while we hold Omaha and the Learning Community as a model of the core elements of the framework that we think is useful, political forces since its inception in 2009 have worked to chip away at key elements of the plan. For example, the tax-base sharing policy was eliminated in April 2016, largely due to suburban resistance, though the regional tax in support of the learning centers still continues. While the interdistrict integration plan has been modified and weakened, two elements of the original legislation are intact: the LCCC governing body, and the elementary learning centers, the in-place strategy which perhaps not surprisingly enjoys the most support given the political dynamics discussed previously, as this does the least to alter the current system and structures. One interviewee lamented the undermining of the Learning Community's goals, observing how the model had potential, but suburban districts worked to undermine this:

> You say, all right, this represents a first step, you have representative governance, you have the potential to do the right thing, now what we're dealing with is the human frailty, we're dealing with the politics of it, we're dealing with the privilege of it, and so if you devote your time avoiding at every opportunity, legitimate discussion about the two primary missions of the Learning Community, you'll continue to wallow. So what we have is an excellent model with wallowing going on.[46]

This observer was optimistic that in putting the regional structure in place, "you at least preserve for the future the opportunity [for] that kind of legitimate conversation about the good of the entire community to be there." In the final chapter, we close by revisiting more directly the politics that get in the way of regional equity and how to overcome them.

SIX

The Politics of Striving
in Common

MANY BOOKS WOULD STOP at the end of chapter 5, having discussed *what* must be done to address the outlined problems. However, as we have suggested throughout this book, the politics of striving in common are no small matter—in fact *how* to get these things done deserves much greater attention in order to facilitate authentic and sustainable progress. The political challenges confronting the policy initiatives we have outlined are significant, but not insurmountable.

We are hopeful that there is increased opportunity to mobilize the political will as a result of significantly increased media coverage of segregation and inequality, combined with the groundswell of social protests by parents and community members (for example, the Black Lives Matter movement) and educators (such as the Detroit public schoolteacher sickouts). However, even with this increased attention to some of the underlying problems stemming from segregated schooling, there is still relatively little understanding about how to bring about broad-based regional equity reforms in education and across the other sectors. Yet the *how* is critical, as political dynamics—and as a result, policies within and outside of education—have for decades served to reinforce the status quo.

As we have argued in this book, both public policy and private actors have created racialized spaces that are, as legal theorist Richard Thompson Ford argues, self-perpetuating in terms of power and inequity. He points out that even with no racist actor or racist policy, a racially stratified society is inevitable due to the ongoing effects of past policies: "Race-neutral policies, set against an historical backdrop of state action in the service of racial segregation and thus against a contemporary backdrop of racially identified space—physical space primarily associated with and occupied by a particular racial group—predictably reproduce and entrench racial segregation and the racial-caste system that accompanies it."[1] This has created a system in which communities are divided and defend their own interests, through either legal or political channels.

Regions that are "strongly divided against themselves"[2] tend to undercut the coalitions necessary to build the types of regional, cross-sector solutions that we outlined in chapter 5. This division manifests itself in localism, supported by political coalitions and interests that are invested in defending the status quo and therefore work against broader regional equity solutions.

In this final chapter, we focus on strategies to interrupt the impact of racialized geography and localism through building support for regional agendas in ways that also support local interests. We discuss key areas of action—including building coalitions, leveraging the work of policy entrepreneurs, redefining the problem, and developing a common vision—and the importance of interest convergence and a focus on race. Along with this, we consider state and federal policies that would boost efforts toward regional equity. We return to Omaha to illustrate some of these points, as this is the single site in our study that is already engaged in the type of broader regional effort that we advocate for.

COALITIONS

As we have discussed in the earlier chapters, civic capacity in a community consists of the connections across individuals and agencies and the resources they bring to bear on social problems.[3] It requires various different sectors in a community to join together in pursuit of solving major problems or challenges.[4] To do so entails the construction of coalitions. As Todd Swanstrom, a professor at the University of Missouri–St. Louis, and his colleagues write: "Civic capacity refers to the ability of a community to build and maintain a broad social and political coalition across all sectors in pursuit of a common goal."[5] A broad-based network of both the elites in the community (including community or business leaders) and a diverse group of citizens is required to develop the political will to move forward and focus on not just deliberation but action.[6] Urban regime theory is useful in understanding how to accomplish this, as it focuses on "the agency of local urban actors who come together in coalitions around reform ideas and bring their independent political, organizational, and economic resources to bear on these commitments."[7]

We found evidence of such coalitions in Omaha, where a network of philanthropists, nonprofits, community activists, and civil rights groups worked in alignment with the newspaper publisher and educational leaders to create change. As an administrator in the Omaha school district pointed out, the regional policy that was enacted would not have been accomplished without the involvement of this coalition of local actors, particularly the advocacy within the philanthropic and civil rights communities:

> There isn't any doubt in my mind that had it not been for the philanthropy component, had it not been for editors in the newspaper, had it not

been for advocacy leaders of this community, had it not been for long-standing institutions that advocated for kids, specifically the NAACP, Chicano Awareness Center, all coming together and saying, as a result of awareness, through understanding, lessons that had been communicated for years, I don't believe for one moment we would be at this point.[8]

While these networks are instrumental in getting reform off the ground, sustaining these policies requires a broader base of political support in local and state governments. The formation of supportive coalitions in state legislatures can be difficult because of the dominance of suburban power,[9] which can undermine regional policy making, as it ultimately did in Omaha, where suburban resistance eventually resulted in significantly scaling back the regional equity initiative.

Indeed, as USC professor Manuel Pastor and colleagues argue, regional movements must go beyond forming horizontal relationships to building a base of power across communities to challenge the status quo. They write that, "if policy reforms are to 'stick'—particularly reforms that can be controversial—mobilization, popular education, and power-building must be part of the equation."[10] Further, as Angela Glover Blackwell and Radhika Fox of Policylink, an organization that is devoted to equity and inclusion, argue, an important coalition-building strategy is through community organizing:

> Regional equity will not fulfill its potential as a movement unless it connects to people in their neighborhoods and daily lives. This is beginning to happen through the work of a growing number of national organizing networks such as Association of Community Organizations for Reform Now (ACORN), Pacific Institute for Community Organization (PICO), and the Gamaliel Foundation. These groups are actively building a base of power in low income communities to advocate for policies addressing the inequitable impact of regional development.[11]

A useful approach can be to build upon the collaborative structures that already exist in communities, for example through the Metropolitan

Planning Organizations. We did not see this as much in our interdistrict plans but we did see it—and it seems particularly critical—in the larger metropolitan efforts toward regional equity.

POLICY ENTREPRENEURS

Promoting a regional equity agenda in any metropolitan community can be challenging given the fragmented self-interests of competitive units (towns, districts, etc.). What can energize or amplify these efforts is a champion, or what is referred to as a "policy entrepreneur."[12] Political scientist John Kingdon has said that policy entrepreneurs "could be in or out of government, in elected or appointed positions, in interest groups or research organizations. But their defining characteristic, much as in the case of a business entrepreneur, is their willingness to invest their resources—time, energy, reputation, and sometimes money—in the hope of a future return."[13]

This entrepreneurship is most likely to be needed when there is a movement toward significant or disruptive change. Indeed, the One City, One School District movement in Omaha created enough turmoil—particularly in the aftermath of the decision—for policy entrepreneurs to emerge and take advantage of the opportunity. As Michael Mintrom and Phillipa Norman of the University of New Zealand write:

> The extant literature suggests that policy entrepreneurship is most likely to be observed in cases where change involves disruption to established ways of doing things . . . Public policies are designed and implemented to address particular problems. Incremental changes are then made to those policies as new challenges arise. However, instances occur when new challenges appear so significant that established systems of managing them are judged inadequate. A key part of policy entrepreneurship involves seizing such moments to promote major change. Such action requires creativity, energy, and political skill.[14]

In Omaha there were several policy entrepreneurs who played key roles in facilitating the creation of the regional policy. Actors like Nebraska state senator Ron Raikes, the Omaha Superintendent John Mackiel, and the publisher of the local newspaper at the time, John Gottschalk, were what Mintrom refers to as creative problem solvers with the networks and persuasive approaches to gain support for new or more controversial policy ideas.[15]

Our research suggests, however, that just getting ideas around regional equity on the policy agenda are not enough. In fact, in many places these policy ideas hang in a tenuous political balance, and as we saw in Omaha, without the original champion or policy entrepreneur involved, the power dynamics can shift toward other players and the reforms can fail. Indeed, the death of Senator Raikes and the retirement of Superintendent Mackiel, along with the changing of the newspaper publisher, created a vacuum in leadership that ultimately contributed to a weakening of the policy. Therefore, ensuring that a core group of champions, not just one or two, are involved and invested can strengthen the sustainability given the political realities.

REDEFINITION OF PROBLEMS

Another critical aspect of change is problem definition, or framing (or more accurately, reframing) the problem of inequality.[16] The key is to help regional players and state actors understand that urban school problems (as well as housing problems, economic development problems, etc.) are the result of regional dynamics rather than the fault of those who struggle (such as urban schools or students).

Our example again comes from Omaha, where education, civic, business, and civil rights advocates worked toward new ways of thinking about long-standing inequities. The critical moment in problem definition came with the Omaha school board's vote to move the school district boundary lines to be contiguous with the city boundary lines, thus annexing a great deal of territory and twenty-five suburban schools in two suburban school districts. This One City, One School District vote brought to light the ways in which segregation and tax-base inequality contributed to the district's problems. As an Omaha Public Schools school board member noted, the school board vote reframed the conversation:

> We defined the problem, we said there's racial isolation, socioeconomic isolation, we don't have the resources to do what we need to do . . . so that it gets to all the children, so we defined the problem. We came up with the policy, where it is we wanted to go, and then we executed it, and we did it without worrying about . . . what our futures would be . . . we said, we're doing it because this is what is best, best for kids, but best for the community.

In this way, the board was able to reframe the dialogue about educational challenges in the region, bringing questions of tax resources, racial isolation, and the distribution of poverty into the policy dialogue, and ultimately catalyzing the regional solution that emerged. The role of the media—in this case the city's major newspaper, the *Omaha World-Herald*—was instrumental here, as it had the capability of shaping policy conversations in the broader community.

COMMON VISION

The ability to engage a community's civic capacity relies on a variety of institutions and individuals who contribute to a shared vision, participate in the change process, and plan to maintain the community over time.[17] In particular, when they operate cooperatively as "urban regimes," governmental and nongovernmental groups are better able to develop long-lasting partnerships and mobilize resources to enact a shared agenda.

Metropolitan Planning Organizations, which as we noted exist in virtually every metropolitan area, form one basis for developing a common vision across a community. In addition, many regions have meetings of school district leaders in the form of regional superintendents' associations, for example; this may be a platform to begin educational conversations that consider both urban and suburban needs as part of larger regional equity goals.

One example we came across is Heartland 2050, the Omaha–Council Bluffs Metropolitan Area Planning Agency's (MAPA) long-term vision plan. As a typical interlocal arrangement, MAPA focuses on transportation, economic development, and environmental issues but it also includes education, housing, and health and safety, and so—at least in theory—is incorporating education into a larger regional approach. We have not found any other regional effort like this that includes education as part of its design. Importantly, Heartland 2050 identifies regional equity at its core, and also has a regional vision for strategies that include people (through jobs, schools, and healthy living), places (through housing and infrastructure), and natural resources. Heartland 2050 has guiding principles of equity, efficiency, and inclusivity. In addition, it emphasizes a balance of both local control and collective vision. "It is critical that cities and counties within the region maintain local control over their communities while also working collectively together to ensure that local decisions enhance rather than adversely affect other neighborhoods, communities, or the region as a whole."[18]

The group worked to develop this common vision through data analysis, as well as in interviews and workshops that involved more than 4,000 people. While city and county government leaders, business leaders, civic and nonprofit agencies, and the general public were reportedly all involved, Heartland 2050 makes it very clear that it has no bonding, taxing, or policy-making authority, and therefore it serves only as a guide to inform leaders. Though this is clearly a limitation, it may be the seeds that could generate a collective vision across a diverse group of individuals and agencies. As Pastor and colleagues point out, regionalism is a way to "lay the groundwork" for new levels of social consciousness.[19]

INTEREST CONVERGENCE

In trying to understand why regional equity has not been embraced in many communities, it is worth reconsidering noted law professor

Derrick Bell's argument from several decades ago regarding the "interest convergence" of African Americans and whites that led to *Brown v. Board of Education*.[20] Bell argued that favorable judicial decisions occur for African Americans only when their interests align with the interests of whites. Though others have argued that convergence theory undercuts the agency of African American citizens and white judges and ultimately limits racial equality,[21] as educational scholar Richard Milner points out, interest convergence theory can be useful 1) as a tool to focus on race, 2) to uncover the ways that policies are positioned in a loss/gain binary, typically with the dominant group giving up something for interests to converge, and 3) to help to explain why "change is often *purposefully* and *skillfully* slow and at the will and design of those in power"[22] (emphasis in original).

Demographic changes in the past several decades, particularly the increased diversity in suburban areas and increasing poverty in suburbs, have created potentially ripe conditions for the formation of new political alliances that allow interests to converge. Inner-ring suburbs are facing fiscal challenges that are often as significant as those facing the urban cores (if not even more so); this creates the potential for urban and inner-ring suburban alliances to work together for change. For example, the tax-base sharing (the common levy) in Omaha was an especially important way to align interests across different types of school districts and the state.[23]

Aligning interests in this way can be difficult, as it often involves working against identity politics. Lower income suburbs often see themselves, despite their shared fiscal problems with core cities, as more suburban, and thus align themselves politically with more affluent suburbs in ways that undermine regional policies.[24] We saw this happen in Omaha, where one lower income suburban community advocated for the dismantling of several key policies that would have aided them in the long run. Thus, regional equity advocacy requires helping suburbs and their representatives see how a regional policy can aid them, and moving the policy dialogue away from a binary or zero-sum perspective (the view that when city families or low income, African American, or Latinx families "win," then affluent, white, or suburban families must "lose") as this prevents interest convergence.[25]

FOCUS ON RACE

Pastor and his colleagues note that the "single most important issue simmering in the regional equity world is race" because, as they point out, "Race, in short, is an inescapable part of America's regional histories, and racism a part of its social institutions."[26] Given the highly racialized geography in metro areas across the country, which we have discussed previously, it is critical that race is not pushed aside as is often done through color-blind policy strategies. The largest costs of regional inequality have been borne historically by the African American and Latinx communities in inner cities and inner-ring suburbs, and these communities are often—for good reason—skeptical of regional approaches. Movements supporting localism and community control of schools have strong roots in communities of color, and many of these communities fought difficult political battles to gain more power and authority in local city governments and within school systems. UC Berkeley professor john powell illustrates the challenge of confronting this skepticism and distrust through his description of a conversation he had with a city school administrator whom he calls Dr. Jones. powell describes how he and Dr. Jones came to an impasse: while powell argued that regional solutions were necessary to address segregation and concentrated poverty, Dr. Jones made it clear that he did not trust the white racists in the suburbs and preferred strengthening the city.[27] As powell notes, understanding the concerns of minority communities around political and cultural control and identity is critical to the success of regional efforts.

Indeed, a benefit of localism for communities of color is that they are able to gain power in local decision making. At the same time, a danger of regionalism, and regional governance structures in particular, is that their hard-fought power and voice can be diffused and weakened if regionalism is not structured to include minority voices.[28] As powell says, to resolve this, a balance must be struck between both regional and local approaches: "The ideal balance between local and regional control will hinge upon recognition of the concerns of communities of color, which require *regional* approaches to address concentrations of poverty and *local* approaches to address the need for political and cultural empowerment."[29]

Federated regionalism helps to address some of these tensions, enabling communities to remain intact along with their governance structures (school boards, city councils, etc.), but with an overarching regional framework that is oriented towards addressing the inequities between them. Any regional effort, however, must be accompanied by a regionally elected board via limited or cumulative voting, which allows the political power of communities of color to be leveraged for representation. Moreover, such an effort has to have a balance between both in-place and mobility policies, to ensure that the choice isn't—as is so often the case—*between* community development and integration for example. Finally, it is critical that developing a common vision and regional agenda integrally involves communities of color to ensure that historical discrimination and power dynamics do not re-emerge.

STATE AND FEDERAL POLICY

Ultimately, states play a critical role in regional equity, as the inequities that exist across regions are under the jurisdiction of the state and must be attended to by state governmental bodies. States like New York—the state that, according to the Civil Rights Project, has the most segregated schools in the country[30]—could begin to tackle these inequities in much the same way they have focused attention on regional economic development. Since 2011, more than $5.4 billion has been awarded across the state to focus on "cooperation and investing in regional assets to generate opportunity."[31] In 2013, Governor Andrew Cuomo presented his "opportunity agenda" to "help poor communities overcome the challenges that prevent them from fully participating in the state's economic revitalization."[32] Ten regional councils across the state competed against each other for resources, but most of the funds targeted toward this effort focused on place-based approaches rather than the regional equity approaches we discussed in chapter 5. A more appropriate way of ensuring that regional equity would be central to this type of competitive grant program would be to include the five components of our framework (tax sharing, place-based approaches, mobility approaches, regional governance, and cross-sector approaches) as heavily weighted criteria for funding.

Encouraging new ways of thinking—and the resulting policies—is critical given competing interests at the local level and a strong push against regional change. Former US Secretary of Education John King's effort to incentivize socioeconomic integration through a pilot program using federal School Improvement Grant funding in 2014 also shows how creative solutions can emerge from this type of incentive, but this effort, as well as the Stronger Together School Diversity Act of 2016 (introduced by Connecticut Senator Chris Murphy and Ohio Congresswoman Marcia Fudge) focused only on education.[33] Similarly, Maryland's recent Commission on Innovation and Excellence in Education recently recommended that the state's school systems "consider strategies for the de-concentration of poverty in schools, using research that shows that beyond a certain level, students learn better in socioeconomically diverse schools."[34] If this recommendation moves forward, it will be important to incorporate components of the equity framework—particularly cross-sector alliances and regional governance—to ensure that regional equity goals remain central to any policy decisions or reallocation of resources.

The federal government has a role to play in using its bully pulpit to orient communities toward regional equity. This was seen in the "Dear Colleagues" letter of June 2016, from the then-secretaries of the Departments of Housing (Julian Castro), Transportation (Anthony R. Foxx), and Education (John B. King) as they called upon their respective constituencies to promote interagency cooperation and planning in local communities. The secretaries stated:

> Today, our agencies are calling on local education, transportation, and housing leaders to work together on issues at the intersection of our respective missions in helping to guarantee full access of opportunity across the country. Our goals are to identify impediments to accessing opportunity; to coordinate efforts to address these issues and to provide broad-reaching benefits; and to ensure that every child and family is provided with transportation, housing, and education tools that promote economic mobility. The new process in which communities are engaging under the Affirmatively Furthering Fair Housing rule (AFFH rule) from HUD provides an opportunity for cross-agency collaboration and strong community involvement. We urge you to take full advantage of the community participation process of the AFFH rule, so that regional planning promotes economic mobility and equal access to the many benefits provided by affordable housing, great schools, and reliable transportation.[35]

In this letter they "encouraged" actions from local agencies and "critical conversations" in communities.

The federal government also has a role to play in using incentives to prompt state or local action. Indeed, as we noted in chapter 4, by building in requirements for regional planning into transit funding, the federal government spurred the creation of hundreds of regional planning agencies across the country (albeit weak and largely focused on transit). Similarly, federal funding could incentivize the development of a regional equity plan that incorporates the five pillars that we outlined. The requirements could be that regions begin by creating a regional governance body or integrating education into its existing regional body, and developing a small tax-base sharing program as critical first steps. The plan would then have to spell out the mobility policies and place-based investments as well as cross-sector approaches that would be implemented as the next steps in pursuit of regional equity goals. To maintain funding, localities must demonstrate meaningful progress.

MOVING FORWARD

The current educational reform approaches have not only been largely ineffective in addressing current patterns of inequality; they have also served to reinforce the idea that educators are both to blame for *and* the only solution to the systematic achievement gaps that affect traditionally marginalized communities. In this book we have argued that these narrowly focused educational policy approaches are akin to using sandbags in an attempt to hold back the powerful waters of inequality. In reality, none of these efforts can be effective unless the larger currents, the power structures that drive these inequalities, are addressed.

In the end, we argue that countering the powerful forces that perpetuate the geography of inequality in education and in other domains (such as housing and economic development) requires addressing the web of forces—economic, political, and personal—that weave together to sustain these inequities. The causes and effects of inequality are regional in nature, and they require a regional solution that is specifically focused on equity across multiple policy domains.

We are at a critical moment in time when years of failed educational reforms, misattribution of the problem, and inattention to historical patterns and social and economic trends have left our educational system more inequitable than ever before. In addition, the country has become increasingly fragmented, as white supremacy runs rampant not just in the far reaches of the country but in our national politics (around immigration, housing, criminal justice, etc.) and economic greed carves out benefits for a small minority of citizens. Growing consideration of how governmental policies have maintained and worsened the inequalities in our country, by allowing economic, educational, and social gains at the expense (once again) of families of color, means that more people are beginning to understand that policy caused these issues and policy must now help to reverse them. We are at a point where we need less attention to narrow reforms and more attention to big ideas that will focus not just on the educational needs of students but on the broader health and economic needs of their families. It is no longer worthwhile to focus narrowly on educational failure without focusing on the broader failures in our society.

As we have repeatedly shown, the political challenges are formidable. Politics, not just policy, must thus be at the center of a regional equity movement that keeps education at its core. Otherwise, as is often the case, well-intentioned visions and goals will not result in purposeful and sustainable actions. This means that it is critical to develop strategies to align interests and examine the ways that the various players can form a diverse coalition and mobilize resources toward collective goals. To do this, regions need continued emphasis on a shared focus on community problems; the development of a broad-based network of elites, community activists, and ordinary citizens involved in deliberation and action; and the mobilization of resources to enact a shared agenda in order to truly "strive together."

NOTES

CHAPTER 1

1. John R. Logan and Brian J. Stults, "The Persistence of Segregation in the Metropolis: Findings from the 2010 Census." *US 2010 Project,* https://s4.ad.brown.edu/Projects/Diveristy/Data/Report/report2.pdf.

2. Missouri Department of Education, "Normandy Schools Collaborative District Report Card," https://mcds.dese.mo.gov/guidedinquiry/Pages/District-and-School-Information.aspx

3. Nikole Hannah-Jones, "562: The Problem We All Live With," July 31, 2015, *This American Life* podcast, https://www.thisamericanlife.org/radio-archives/episode/562/the-problem-we-all-live-with.

4. Stanton Lawrence (former superintendent, Normandy School District), in discussion with the author, February 2018; Stanton Lawrence, "How Missouri Killed the Normandy School District," *Diane Ravitch Blog,* https://dianeravitch.net/2014/06/22/stanton-lawrence-how-missouri-killed-the-normandy-school-district/.

5. Lawrence, interview.

6. Victoria Johnson, "St. Louis Education Inequality: Normandy," *Washington University Political Review,* March 23, 2016, http://www.wupr.org/2016/03/23/st-louis-education-inequality-normandy/.

7. Nikole Hannah-Jones, "562: The Problem We All Live With."

8. Missouri Department of Elementary and Secondary Education, "Normandy Schools Collaborative to Operate with New Leadership," June 16, 2004, https://dese.mo.gov/communications/news-releases/normandy-schools-collaborative-operate-new-leadership; Dale Singer, "Judge Rules Normandy Schools Unaccredited," St. Louis Public Radio, February 12, 2015, http://news.stlpublicradio.org/post/judge-rules-normandy-schools-unaccredited#stream/0.

9. Kenneth T. Jackson, *Crabgrass Frontier: The Suburbanization of the United States* (New York: Oxford University Press, 1987).

10. Myron Orfield, *American Metropolitics: The New Suburban Reality* (Washington, DC: The Urban Institute Press, 2002).

11. "The Will to Change," *Better Together St. Louis,* http://www.bettertogetherstl.com/studies/will-to-change.

12. Lawrence, interview.
13. "A Preservation Plan for St. Louis Part I: Historic Contexts," City of St. Louis, MO: Official Website, https://www.stlouis-mo.gov/government/departments/planning /cultural-resources/preservation-plan/Part-I-African-American-Experience.cfm.
14. Colin Gordon, *Mapping Decline: Saint Louis and the Fate of the American City* (Philadelphia: University of Pennsylvania Press, 2008), 104.
15. Gordon, *Mapping Decline.*
16. In these maps, we elected to focus on only Latinos and African Americans (in comparison to whites) because of the large-scale impact segregation has had on these communities. In addition, these two racial/ethnic subgroups are the largest racial minority groups in the cities we studied. Both Asian and Pacific Islander and Native Americans were not included in our mapping analysis because of the relatively smaller numbers in each city.
17. US Census, "Per Capita Income, 2010–2014," *American Community Survey.*
18. "Tax Rates," St. Louis County, http://revenue.stlouisco.com/collection/yourtaxrates .aspx.
19. Orfield, *American Metropolitics.*
20. Richard Bose, "As Wealth and Residents Flee, St. Louis County Munis Turn to Fines and Fees," *NextSTL,* https://nextstl.com/2014/11/wealth-residents-flee-st-louis -county-munis-turn-fines-fees/.
21. John L. Rury and Argun Saatcioglu, "Suburban Advantage: Opportunity Hoarding and Secondary Attainment in the Postwar Metropolitan North," *American Journal of Education* 117, no. 3 (2011), 307–342.
22. This analogy is also made by Myron Orfield in *American Metropolitics.*
23. Emma Brown. "In 23 States, Richer School Districts Get More Local Funding Than Poorer Districts," *The Washington Post,* https://www.washingtonpost.com/news/local /wp/2015/03/12/in-23-states-richer-school-districts-get-more-local-funding-than -poorer-districts/?utm_term=.5e137af27763.
24. Orfield, *American Metropolitics,* 72.
25. *Edging Toward Equity,* Report from the Conversation on Regional Equity (CORE), 2006, 5, http://cjtc.ucsc.edu/regionalequity.html, as cited in Manuel Pastor, Jr., Chris Benner, and Martha Matsuoka, *This Could Be the Start of Something Big: How Social Movements for Regional Equity Are Reshaping Metropolitan America* (Ithaca, NY: Cornell University Press, 2009), 25.
26. Paul Kantor, "The End of American Urban Policy—or the Beginning," *Urban Affairs Review* (2015): 908, doi:10.1177/1078087415617550.
27. The community schools movement is one important exception to recent reform debates.
28. A notable exception is the insightful book by Genevieve Siegel-Hawley, *When the Fences Come Down: Twenty-First-Century Lessons from Metropolitan School Desegregation* (Chapel Hill: The University of North Carolina Press, 2016).
29. Marion Orr and Valerie C. Johnson, "Power and Local Democracy: Clarence N. Stone and American Political Science," in *Power in the City,* eds. Marion Orr and Valerie C. Johnson (Lawrence: University Press of Kansas, 2008).
30. Richard Thompson Ford, "The Boundaries of Race: Political Geography in Legal Analysis," in *In Pursuit of a Dream Deferred: Linking Housing and Education Policy,*

ed. john a. powell, Gavin Kearney, and Vina Kay (New York: Peter Lang, 2001), 236.

31. Rury and Saatcioglu, "Suburban Advantage."

32. Dorothy Shipps, "Pulling Together: Civic Capacity and Urban School Reform," *American Educational Research Journal* 40, no. 4 (2003): 841–878, doi:10.3102 /00028312040004841; Peter Burns, "The Intergovernmental Regime and Public Policy in Hartford, Connecticut," *Journal of Urban Affairs* 24 (2002): 55–73, doi:10 .1111/1467-9906.00114; Dana L. Mitra and William C. Frick, "Civic Capacity in Educational Reform Efforts: Emerging and Established Regimes in Rust Belt Cities," *Educational Policy* 25 (2011): 810–843, doi:10.1177/0895904810386597; Katrina E. Bulkley, "Bringing the Private into the Public: Changing the Rules of the Game and New Regime Politics in Philadelphia Public Education," *Educational Policy* 21 (2007): 155–184, doi:10.1177/0895904806297192.

33. Karen Mossberger and Gerry Stoker, "The Evolution of Urban Regime Theory: The Challenge of Conceptualization," *Urban Affairs Review* 36, no. 6 (2001): 810–835, doi:10.1177/10780870122185109.

34. Marion Orr and Valerie C. Johnson, *Power in the City* (Lawrence: University Press of Kansas, 2008); Clarence N. Stone, Jeffrey R. Henig, Bryan D. Jones, and Carol Pierannunzi, *Building Civic Capacity: The Politics of Reforming Urban Schools* (Lawrence: University Press of Kansas, 2001); Jeffrey R. Henig, Richard C. Hula, Marion Orr, and Desiree S. Pedelescleaux, *The Color of School Reform: Race, Politics and the Challenge of Urban Education* (Princeton, NJ: Princeton University Press, 1999).

35. Stone, Henig, Jones, and Pierannunzi, *Building Civic Capacity*.

36. Robert J. Chaskin, Prudence Brown, Sudhir Venkatesh, and Avid Vidal, *Building Community Capacity* (New York: Aldine, 2001); Dana L. Mitra, William C. Frick, and Marcela A. Movit, "Brain Drain in the Rust Belt: Can Educational Reform Help to Build Civic Capacity in Struggling Communities?" *Educational Policy* 22 (2008): 731–757, doi: 10.1177/0895904807310038; John Portz, Lana Stein, and Robin R. Jones, *City Schools and City Politics* (Lawrence: University Press of Kansas, 1999).

37. Clarence N. Stone, *Regime Politics: Governing Atlanta, 1946–1988*, (Lawrence: University Press of Kansas, 1989).

38. See, for example, Stefanie DeLuca, Susan Clampet-Lundquist, and Kathryn Edin, *Coming of Age in the Other America* (New York: Russell Sage Foundation, 2016); Raj Chetty, Nathaniel Hendren, and Lawrence F. Katz, "The Effects of Exposure to Better Neighborhoods on Children: New Evidence from the Moving to Opportunity Experiment," *American Economic Review* (2015), doi:10.1257/aer.20150572; Robert J. Sampson, *Great American City: Chicago and The Enduring Neighborhood Effect* (Chicago: University of Chicago Press, 2012); Patrick Sharkey, *Stuck in Place: Urban Neighborhoods and the End of Progress Toward Racial Equity* (Chicago: University of Chicago Press, 2013).

CHAPTER 2

1. "Wisconsin Department of Public Instruction, 2015–16 District Report Card," https://dpi.wi.gov/accountability/report-cards.

2. Wisconsin District Report Card.

3. Alberta Darling, "Sen Darling: Why Won't Leaders Stand Up for Kids?" McIver Institute, Sept 12, 2016, http://www.maciverinstitute.com/2016/09/sen-darling-why -wont-milwaukees-leaders-stand-up-for-kids/.

4. James Wigderson, "Kooyenga: Break Up of Milwaukee Public Schools on the Table," Watchdog.org, June 30, 2016, http://watchdog.org/269598/breakup-of-mps-possible/.

5. For an example, see Dakarai I. Aarons, "Decline and Fall," *Education Week,* July 31, 2009, http://www.edweek.org/ew/articles/2009/07/31/37detroit.h28.html; "US Secretary of Education to Mayor: KC Schools Worst in Nation," KCTV, http://www.kctv5.com/story/16455090/us-edcuation-secretary-to-mayor-kc-schools-worst-in-nation.

6. Molly Beck, "Betsy DeVos Tied to Millions Spent in Wisconsin Politics," *The Journal Times*, January 18, 2017, http://journaltimes.com/news/state-and-regional/betsy-devos-tied-to-millions-spent-in-wisconsin-politics/article_a906a97e-1871-5bd5-9a02-8a76b633160d.html.

7. Annysa Johnson, "School Voucher Programs Grow in 2015–16," *Milwaukee Journal Sentinel,* October 24, 2010, http://www.jsonline.com/story/news/education/2016/10/24/school-voucher-programs-grow-2015-16/92684598/; Erin Richards, "Study Shows Charters Outpacing Traditional Milwaukee Schools," *Milwaukee Journal Sentinel,* March 18, 2015, http://archive.jsonline.com/news/education/study-shows-charters-modestly-outpacing-traditional-milwaukee-schools-b99464902z1-296798931.html

8. john a. powell, "Opportunity is Racialized," FORA tv, http://library.fora.tv/2009/09/07/POWER_john_a_powell_on_Opportunity_and_Race

9. James E. Ryan, Five Miles Away, A World Apart: One City, Two Schools, and the Story of Educational Opportunity in Modern America (New York: Oxford University Press, 2010).

10. sean f. reardon, "School Segregation and Racial Academic Achievement Gaps," *The Russell Sage Foundation Journal of the Social Sciences* 2, no. 5 (2015); Ann Owens, sean f. reardon, and Christopher Jencks, "Income Segregation Between Schools and School Districts," *American Educational Research Journal* 53, no. 4 (2014): 1159–1197. http://journals.sagepub.com/doi/full/10.3102/0002831216652722; Gary Orfield, Genevieve Siegel-Hawley, and John Kucsera, *Sorting Out Deepening Confusion on Segregation Trends*, UCLA Civil Rights Project (2014).

11. Anthony S. Bryk et al., *Organizing Schools for Improvement: Lessons from Chicago* (Chicago: University of Chicago Press, 2010).

12. Douglas N. Harris, "High Flying Schools, Student Disadvantage, and the Logic of NCLB," *American Journal of Education* 113 (2007).

13. reardon, "School Segregation"; Geoffrey Borman and Maritza Dowling, "Schools and Inequality: A Multilevel Analysis of Coleman's Equality of Educational Opportunity Data," *Teachers College Record* 112, no. 5 (2008): 1201–1246; Russell W. Rumberger and Gregory J. Palardy, "Does Segregation Still Matter? The Impact of Student Composition on Academic Achievement in High School," *Teachers College Record 107,* no. 9 (2005): 1999–2045.

14. reardon, "School Segregation."

15. Rumberger and Palardy, "Does Segregation Still Matter?"

16. sean f. reardon and Ann Owens, "60 years after *Brown*: Trends and Consequences of School Segregation," *Annual Review of Sociology* 40 (2014).

17. Sonya Douglass Horsford, *Learning in a Burning House: Educational Inequality, Ideology and (Dis)Integration* (New York: Teachers College Press, 2011).

18. Amanda Lewis and John Diamond, *Despite the Best Intentions: How Racial Inequality Thrives in Good Schools* (New York: Oxford University Press, 2017).

19. Richard Rothstein, "For Public Schools, Segregation Then, Segregation Since: Education and the Unfinished March," *Economic Policy Institute* (2013), http://www.epi.org/publication/unfinished-march-public-school-segregation/.

20. Richard Rothstein, *The Color of Law: A Forgotten History of How Our Government Segregated America* (New York: W.W. Norton, 2017).

21. Douglas S. Massey and Nancy A. Denton, *American Apartheid: Segregation and the Making of the Underclass* (Cambridge, MA: Harvard University Press, 1993).

22. Massey and Denton, *American Apartheid,* 26.

23. Massey and Denton, *American Apartheid.*

24. These restrictions also applied to Jews and other nonwhites.

25. *Buchanan v. Warley,* 245 U.S. 60 (1917).

26. Eliot M. Tretter, "Austin Restricted: Progressivism, Zoning, Private Racial Covenants, and the Making of a Segregated City," *The University of Texas at Austin* (2012), https://repositories.lib.utexas.edu/handle/2152/21232.

27. Jon C. Teaford, *City and Suburb: The Political Fragmentation of Metropolitan America 1850–1970* (Baltimore: Johns Hopkins University Press, 1979), 58.

28. Margaret Weir, "Central Cities' Loss of Power in State Politics," *Cityscape: A Journal of Urban Development* 2, (1996), 157. According to Weir, in 1950 the city of Chicago contained nearly 70 percent and New York City nearly 80 percent of the residents in their respective metro areas.

29. Beginning in the early twentieth century, cities would be less successful in annexations, annexing only the economically weakest suburbs, while the wealthiest suburbs would remain autonomous. Teaford, *City and Suburb,* 90.

30. John L. Rury, *Seeds of Crisis: Public Schooling in Milwaukee Since 1920* (Madison: University of Wisconsin Press, 1993), 24.

31. Clarence Stone, *Changing Urban Education* (Lawrence: University Press of Kansas, 1998), 4.

32. David Tyack, *The One Best System: A History of American Urban Education* (Cambridge, MA: Harvard University Press, 1974).

33. Stone, *Changing Urban Education,* 5.

34. This stands in sharp contrast to expectations for urban districts today, which are expected, in public rhetoric and policies like the Every Student Succeeds Act, to bring all students to the same level of performance.

35. Jeannie Oakes, Amy Stuart Wells, Makeba Jones, and Amanda Datnow, "Detracking: The Social Construction of Ability, Cultural Politics, and Resistance to Reform," *Teachers College Record* 98 (2007): 482–510.

36. Kathryn M. Neckerman, *Schools Betrayed: Roots of Failure in Inner-City Education* (Chicago: University of Chicago Press, 2007).

37. Massey and Denton, *American Apartheid,* 53.

38. These practices had been encoded into federal policy by the federal Home Owners Loan Corporation, established in 1933.

39. These laws were first enacted in the mid-1800s, when many states adopted laws that allowed cities to incorporate relatively easily, without having to appeal individual cases to the states.

40. Kenneth Jackson, *Crabgrass Frontier: The Suburbanization of the United States* (New York: Oxford University Press, 1985).

41. Teaford, *City and Suburb*, 38; Jackson, *Crabgrass Frontier*.

42. Teaford, *City and Suburb*, 77.

43. Teaford, *City and Suburb*, 77.

44. "Annexation," City of Houston, http://www.houstontx.gov/planning/Annexation/

45. Teaford, *City and Suburb*, 77.

46. Massey and Denton, *American Apartheid*, 45.

47. David Tyack, *The One Best System: A History of American Urban Education* (Cambridge, MA: Harvard University Press, 1974), 278.

48. Jarod Apperson, "An Afterward to White Flight: Atlanta's Return to Community and Long Road Toward Integration," *East Atlanta Patch,* http://patch.com/georgia/east atlanta/bp--an-afterward-to-white-flight-atlantas-return-to-cd126722ab4.

49. Massey and Denton, *American Apartheid*, 45.

50. David G. Gutiérrez, "An Historic Overview of Latino Immigration and the Demographic Transformation of the United States," National Park Service, https://www .nps.gov/heritageinitiatives/latino/latinothemestudy/immigration.htm.

51. Jon C. Teaford, *The Metropolitan Revolution: The Rise of Post-Urban America* (New York: Columbia University Press, 2006), 127. Between 1960 and 1970, Memphis *would* have declined by 11,000 if it had not annexed the outlying Shelby county municipalities; the school systems, however, stayed separate, with important implications for the future.

52. Teaford, *Metropolitan Revolution*.

53. Ryan, *Five Miles Away*.

54. Massey and Denton, *American Apartheid*.

55. William J. Collins and Robert A. Margo, "Labor Market Effects of the 1960s Riots," *National Bureau of Economic Research* (working paper, National Bureau of Economic Research, 2004), http://www.nber.org/papers/w10243.

56. Gary Orfield, "Race and the Liberal Agenda: The Loss of the Integrationist Dream, 1965–1974," in *The Politics of Social Policy in the United States,* ed. Margaret Weir et al. (Princeton, NJ: Princeton University Press, 1988), 313–356.

57. One such example is Detroit, where the white population declined both numerically and proportionately, while the African American population grew from 45.8 percent African American to 63.6 percent African American between 1960 and 1970. The overall African American population in Detroit public schools rose from 131,000 to 184,000 between 1960 and 1970 as well. See *Bradley v. Milliken*, 338 F. Supp. 582 (E.D. Mich. 1971).

58. *Green v. County School Board of New Kent County*, 391 U.S. 430 (1968); *Swann v. Charlotte-Mecklenburg Board of Education*, 402 U.S. 1 (1971).

59. *Milliken v. Bradley*, 418 U.S. 717 (1974)

60. *San Antonio Independent School District v. Rodriguez*, 411 U.S. 1 (1973).

61. Orfield, "Race and the Liberal Agenda," 359.

62. Jeffery R. Henig et al., *The Color of School Reform: Race, Politics, and the Challenge of Urban Education*, (Princeton, NJ: Princeton University Press, 2001), 55.

63. Rury, *Seeds of Crisis*, 27.

64. Henig, *The Color of School Reform*, 52.

65. Amy Stuart Wells, Jennifer Jellison Holme, Anita Revilla, and Awo Korantemaa, "How Society Failed School Desegregation Policy: Looking Past the Schools to Understand Them," *Review of Research in Education,* 28 (2004): 47–99.

66. Harvey Kantor and Robert Lowe, "Educationalizing the Welfare State and Privatizing Education: The Evolution of Social Policy Since the New Deal," in *Closing the Opportunity Gap: What America Must Do to Give Every Child an Even Chance,* ed. Prudence L. Carter and Kevin G. Welner (New York: Oxford University Press, 2013), 11.

67. Kantor and Lowe, "Educationalizing the Welfare State." Indeed, as Harvey Kantor and Robert Lowe argue, ESEA was initially not strongly supported by African American groups, who saw it as a way to promote "separate but equal" schooling. Some historians argue that ESEA and other great society programs were in fact meant to dampen African Americans' "demands for more integration." Yet, while the ESEA did not address school segregation directly, federal officials did threaten to withhold funding from school districts that refused to integrate. Harve Kantor and Robert Lowe, "Class, Race, and the Emergence of Federal Education Policy: From the New Deal to the Great Society," *Educational Researcher,* 24 (1995): 5.

68. In the 1970s and 1980s, the Effective Schools movement grew in popularity, and by 1989, the GAO found that 41 percent of districts surveyed had effective schools programs in operation. The principles of the movement also became embodied in federal educational policy through the 1988 amendments to ESEA.

69. Russ Kava, *School Integration (Chapter 220) Aid (Informational Paper 25)*, Wisconsin Legislative Fiscal Bureau (2013), 1.

70. Gary Orfield and Susan E. Eaton, *Dismantling Desegregation: The Quiet Reversal of Brown v. Board of Education* (New York: The New Press, 1996), 90-93.

71. For example, in Detroit, the declining tax base along with opposition to raising taxes resulted in a deep financial crisis—the district dropped from 44th in the state in per pupil expenditures in 1966/67 to 93rd by 1985/86; teacher salaries went from 12th in the state in 1966/67 to 104th in 1985/86. See Jeffery Mirel, *The Rise and Fall of an Urban School System: Detroit, 1907–91* (Ann Arbor: University of Michigan Press, 1999), 359.

72. sean f. reardon and Kendra Bischoff, "Income Inequality and Income Segregation," *American Journal of Sociology,* 116 (2001): 32.

73. Myron Orfield, *American Metropolitics: The New Suburban Reality* (Washington, DC: Brookings Institution Press, 2002); Ann Owens, "Inequality in Children's Contexts: Income Segregation of Households With and Without Children," *American Sociological Review* 81, no. 3 (2016): 549–574.

74. Peter Moscowitz, *How to Kill a City: Gentrification, Inequality, and the Fight for the Neighborhood* (New York: Nation Books, 2017); see also "Governing: Gentrification in America Report," http://www.governing.com/gov-data/census/gentrification-in-cities-governing-report.html#citieslist.

75. Owens, reardon, and Jencks, "Income Segregation," 1159.

76. Owens, "Inequality in Children's Contexts."

77. Kara S. Finnigan, Catherine Bitter, and Jennifer O'Day, "Improving Low-Performing Schools Through External Assistance: Lessons from Chicago and California," *Education Policy Analysis Archives* 17, no. 7 (2009), http://epaa.asu.edu/epaa/v17n7.; Kara S. Finnigan and Bethany Gross, "Do Accountability Policy Sanctions Influence

Teacher Motivation? Lessons from Chicago's Low-Performing Schools," *American Educational Research Journal*, 44, no. 3 (2007): 594–629.

78. William J. Mathis and Tina Trujillo, "Lessons from NCLB for the Every Student Succeeds Act. Boulder, CO: National Education Policy Center," National Education Policy Center (2016), http://nepc.colorado.edu/publication/lessons-from-NCLB.

79. Kara S. Finnigan and Betheny Gross, "Do Accountability Policy Sanctions Influence Teacher Motivation? Lessons from Chicago's Low-Performing Schools," *American Educational Research Journal* 44, no. 3 (2007): 594–629.

80. "Fifty-State Comparison: Charter School Policies," Education Commission of the States, https://www.ecs.org/charter-school-policies/.

81. Joe Nathan, *Charter Schools: Creating Hope and Opportunity for American Education* (San Francisco: Jossey-Bass, 1996).

82. Jennifer Jellison Holme and Amy Stuart Wells, "School Choice Beyond District Borders: Lessons for the Reauthorization of NCLB from Interdistrict Desegregation and Open Enrollment Plans," in *Improving on No Child Left Behind,* ed. Richard Kahlenberg (New York: The Century Foundation Press, 2008), 139–215.

83. Katrina E. Bulkley, Jeffrey R. Henig, and Henry M. Levin, *Between Public and Private: Politics, Governance, and the New Portfolio Models for Urban School Reform* (Cambridge, MA: Harvard University Press, 2010).

84. sean f. reardon et al., "Left Behind? The Effect of No Child Left Behind on Academic Achievement Gaps," *Stanford Center for Education Public Analysis* (2013); Erica Frankenberg, Genevieve Siegel-Hawley, and Jia Wang, "Charter Without Equity: Charter School Segregation," *Education Policy Analysis Archives* 19, no. 1 (2011).

85. Indeed, in the Milwaukee Public Schools a large number of schools are designated as "failing" (or "Schools Identified For Improvement"). In recent years, the number of such schools actually *increased* from forty-eight in 2013/14, to fifty-five in 2014/15.

86. For more details, including trends in changes over time in racial and income segregation in Milwaukee between 1970 and 2012, see Kara S. Finnigan, Jennifer Jellison Holme, and Joanna Sanchez, "Regional Equity as an Educational Policy Goal: Tackling the Root Cause of Educational 'Failure,'" *Education Law and Policy Review* 3, (2016): 166–208.

87. One study found that during the 2007/8 school year, 67 percent of the nearly 4,000 open enrollment transfers out of Milwaukee were white. Michael Bonds, Marie G. Sandy, and Raquel L. Farmer-Hinton, "The Rise and Fall of a Voluntary Public School Integration Transportation Program: A Case Study of Milwaukee's 220 Program," *Education and Urban Society*, 47 (2013): 17.

88. John L. Rury and Argun Saatcioglu, "Suburban Advantage: Opportunity Hoarding and Secondary Attainment in the Postwar Metropolitan North," *American Journal of Education*, 117 (2011).

CHAPTER 3

1. Elizabeth Lorenz, "Tinsley Settlement Was a Decade in the Making," Palo Alto Online, October 7, 1998, https://www.paloaltoonline.com/weekly/morgue/cover/1998_Oct_7.COVSIDE1.html; see *Tinsley v. Palo Alto Unified School District, State of California, et al.* (1976, appealed 1979).

2. Jessica Bernstein-Wax and Diana Samuels, "Tinsley Program Still Attracting Students 22 Years Later," *San Jose Mercury News*, 2010, https://www.mercurynews.com/2010/02/23/tinsley-program-still-attracting-students-22-years-later/.

3. *Tinsley v. Palo Alto Unified School District, State of California, et al.* No. 206010 Settlement Order (Superior Court of the State of California, County of San Mateo, 1986).

4. Suburban school districts were allowed to exit the program (and to stop receiving Ravenswood transfer students) if more than 60 percent of their student populations were students of color; due to this provision, Redwood City was removed from the requirements of the settlement in 1994.

5. Kara S. Finnigan et al., "Regional Educational Policy Analysis: Rochester, Omaha, and Minneapolis' Inter-District Arrangements," *Educational Policy* 29, no. 5 (2014): 1–35, doi:10.1177/0895904813518102.

6. Finnigan et al., "Regional Educational Policy Analysis"; Amy Stuart Wells et al., "Boundary Crossing for Diversity, Equity, and Achievement: Inter-District School Desegregation and Educational Opportunity," Charles Hamilton Houston Institute for Race and Justice (2009), https://sheffmovement.org/wp-content/uploads/2014/04/Wells_BoundaryCrossing.pdf.

7. See Jonathan Guryan, "Desegregation and Black Dropout Rates," *The American Economic Review* 94, no. 4 (2004); Rucker Johnson, *Long-Run Impacts of School Desegregation and School Quality on Adult Attainments* (Cambridge, MA: National Bureau of Economic Research, 2011); sean f. reardon and Ann Owens, "Sixty years after *Brown*: Trends and Consequences of School Segregation," *Annual Review of Sociology* 40 (2014); Heather Schwartz, *Housing Policy Is School Policy: Economically Integrative Housing Promotes Academic Success in Montgomery County, Maryland* (New York: The Century Foundation, 2010); Amy Stuart Wells, Jennifer Jellison Holme, Anita Revilla, and Awo Korantemaa Atanda, *Both Sides Now: The Story of Desegregation's Graduates* (Berkeley: The University of California Press, 2009). Amy Stuart Wells and Robert L. Crain, *Steppin' Over the Color Line: African American Students in White Suburban Schools* (New Haven, CT: Yale University Press, 1999); Susan E. Eaton, *The Other Boston Busing Story: What's Won and Lost Across the Boundary Line* (New Haven, CT: Yale University Press, 2001); Joshua D. Angrist and Kevin Lang, "Does School Integration Generate Peer Effects? Evidence from Boston," *The American Economic Review* 94, no. 5 (2004): 1613–1634; Aspen Associates, *Minnesota Voluntary Public School Choice, Multi-Year Evaluation Summary* (Minneapolis: Minnesota Dept. of Education, 2009); Robert Bifulco, Casey Cobb, and Courtney Bell, "Can Interdistrict Choice Boost Student Achievement? The Case of Connecticut's Interdistrict Magnet School Program," *Educational Evaluation and Policy Analysis* 31, no. 4 (2009); Robert L. Crain and Jack Strauss, *School Desegregation and Black Occupational Attainment: Results from a Long-Term Experiment* (Baltimore: Johns Hopkins University Press, 1985); Harold M. Rose and Diane Pollard, *Interdistrict Chapter 220: Changing Goals and Perspectives* (Milwaukee, WI: Public Policy Forum, 2000); Kendra Bischoff, "Negotiating Disparate Social Contexts: Evidence from an Interdistrict School Desegregation Program" (PhD diss., Stanford University, 2011).

8. Finnigan et al., "Regional Educational Policy Analysis."

9. Bayinaah R. Jones, "The Tinsley Case Decision" (PhD diss, University of North Carolina at Chapel Hill, 2006).

10. Rhonda Rigenhagen, *A History of East Palo Alto* (East Palo Alto: Romic Chemical Corporation, 1993).

11. Rigenhagen, *A History of East Palo Alto.*

12. Jones, "The Tinsley Case Decision."

13. Michael Kahan, "Reading Whiskey Gulch: The Meanings of Space and Urban Redevelopment in East Palo Alto," *Occasion*, special issue on Race, Space, and Scale, ed. Wendy Cheng and Rashad Shabazz, 8 (2015): 7.

14. Albert Camarillo, "Cities of Color: The New Racial Frontier in California's Minority Majority Cities," *Pacific Historical Review* 76, no. 1 (2007): 1–28.

15. Kahan, "Reading Whiskey Gulch."

16. Kim Mai-Cutler, "East of Palo Alto's Eden: Race and the Formation of Silicon Valley," *Tech Crunch*, January 10, 2015, https://techcrunch.com/2015/01/10/east-of -palo-altos-eden/.

17. Tracy Jan, "Ravenswood revisited, reunited," Palo Alto Online, September 11, 1996, https://www.paloaltoonline.com/weekly/morgue/cover/1996_Sep_11.COVER11.html

18. Russell Rickford, *We Are an African People: Independent Education, Black Power, and the Radical Imagination* (New York: Oxford University Press, 2016), 110.

19. Robert Lowe, "Ravenswood High School and the Struggle for Racial Justice in Sequoia Union High School" (PhD diss., Stanford University, 1989), as cited in Rickford, *We Are an African People*, 106.

20. Rickford, *We Are an African People.*

21. Dara Kerr, "East Palo Alto: Life on the Other Side of Silicon Valley's Tracks," CNET, August 31, 2015, https://www.cnet.com/news/east-palo-alto-life-on-the-other-side -of-silicon-valleys-tracks/.

22. *Tinsley v. Palo Alto.*

23. Bischoff, "Negotiating Disparate Social Contexts."

24. Bischoff, "Negotiating Disparate Social Contexts," 71.

25. Ravenswood City School District, http://www.ravenswoodschools.org/about.html

26. Ravenswood City Elementary, 2016/17 calculation of free and reduced-price meals, http://www.ed-data.org/district/San-Mateo/Ravenswood-City-Elementary.

27. Kahan, "Reading Whiskey Gulch," 1.

28. Kahan, "Reading Whiskey Gulch," 7.

29. Queenie Wong, "Menlo Park East Palo Alto Residents to Rally Against Amazon and Facebook Amid Gentrification Concerns," *Mercury News*, March 30, 2017. Note: Amazon appears to have negotiated this specialist role, in lieu of giving a good-faith effort toward hiring 30 percent of employees from within the city as required by city policy.

30. Kerr, "East Palo Alto: Life on the Other Side."

31. Mai-Cutler, "East of Palo Alto's Eden."

32. Bischoff, "Negotiating Disparate Social Contexts."

33. Elena Kadvany, "Ravenswood Faces Financial Crisis," Palo Alto Online, January 26, 2018, https://www.paloaltoonline.com/news/2018/01/26/ravenswood-faces-financial -crisis.

34. "Rochester-Monroe Anti-Poverty Initiative" United Way of Rochester, *Progress Report: A Roadmap for Change,* September 2015, https://www.uwrochester.org/UWGR /media/Connect/RMAPI_progress-report_readers_spreads_lowres_5.pdf.

35. Retrieved from Rochester City School District Enrollment, NYSED Data Site, https://data.nysed.gov/enrollment.php?year=2016&instid=800000050065.

36. Retrieved from State and County Quick Facts tool of the US Census Bureau, https://www.census.gov/quickfacts/fact/table/US/PST045217.

37. Joe Campbell and Meaghan McDermott, "Rochester Graduation Rate Improves, But Still Lags State Average," *Democrat and Chronicle*, February 10, 2017; Joseph Spector and Justin Murphy, "Student Test Scores Inch Up; Opt Outs Down," *Democrat and Chronicle*, August 22, 2017.

38. Mark Hare, "Riots Still Haunt Rochester," *Rochester City Newspaper*, July 16, 2014, https://www.rochestercitynewspaper.com/rochester/riots-still-haunt-rochester/Content?oid=2408308.

39. James Goodman, "1964 Riots Revisited: 3 Days That Shook Rochester," *Democrat and Chronicle,* July 20, 2014, http://www.democratandchronicle.com/story/news/2014/07/19/roberta-abbott-buckle-rochester-riots/12855941/; Mark Hare, "Riots Still Haunt Rochester."

40. West Irondequoit Newsletter (Number 37, April 1965).

41. Amanda E. Lewis and John B. Diamond, *Despite the Best Intentions: How Racial Inequality Thrives in Good Schools,* Transgressing Boundaries: Studies in Black Politics and Black Communities (New York: Oxford University Press, 2015).

42. One of the districts has since stopped taking students.

43. Chyna Stephens, "Essay: Misperceptions on Urban Suburban," *Democrat and Chronicle*, December 7, 2014, http://www.democratandchronicle.com/story/opinion/guest-column/2014/12/07/urban-suburban-rochester-chyna-stevens/20040467/.

44. Justin Murphy, "Spencerport Urban-Suburban Debate," *Democrat and Chronicle,* December 9, 2014, http://www.democratandchronicle.com/story/news/2014/12/09/spencerport-urban-suburban-debate/20172821/.

45. Quinisha Anderson, "I'm Sorry, Future Spencerport Urban-Suburban Students," *Democrat and Chronicle,* December 11, 2014, http://www.democratandchronicle.com/story/unite/2014/12/11/im-sorry-future-spencerport-urban-suburban-students/20278925/.

46. Tim Louis Macaluso, "Standing Up for City Schools," *City Newspaper*, May 27, 2015.

47. Tiffany Lankes, "Watchdog Report: Schools in Black and White," *Democrat and Chronicle*, October 27, 2013.

48. "Rochester-Monroe Anti-Poverty Initiative."

49. Patti Singer, "RMAPI to Give Update on Mentoring Programs," *Democrat and Chronicle,* May 15, 2017, http://www.democratandchronicle.com/story/news/2017/05/15/rmapi-give-update-mentoring-programs/101707894/.

50. See *Brewer v. West Irondequoit Central School District*, http://caselaw.findlaw.com/us-2nd-circuit/1014190.html.

CHAPTER 4

1. Scott A. Bollens, "In Through the Back Door: Social Equity and Regional Governance," *Housing Policy Debate* 13, no. 4 (2002): 631.

2. "History of the Met Council," Met Council, https://metrocouncil.org/Publications-Resources-NEW.aspx.

3. Myron Orfield, *Metropolitics: A Regional Agenda for Community and Stability* (Washington, DC: Brookings Institution Press, 1997). See also Myron Orfield, "Politics and Regionalism" in *Urban Sprawl: Causes, Consequences, and Policy Responses*, ed. G. D. Squires (Washington, DC: Urban Institute Press, 2002), 237–254.

4. Orfield, "Politics and Regionalism," 239.

5. Orfield, *Metropolitics*; Myron Orfield, *St. Louis Metropolitics: A Regional Agenda for Community and Stability* (Minneapolis: Metropolitan Area Research Corporation, 1999).

6. Dennis R. Judd and Todd Swanstrom, *City Politics: The Political Economy of Urban America* (New York: Longman Press, 2010); Ronald K. Vogel and John J. Harrigan, *Political Change in The Metropolis* (New York: Pearson Education, 2007).

7. Fragmentation is defined by Kendra Bischoff as the "proliferation of autonomous jurisdictions." See Kendra Bischoff, "School District Fragmentation and Racial Residential Segregation: How Do Boundaries Matter?" *Urban Affairs Review* 44 (2008): 182.

8. Jeffrey M. Sellers, "Metropolitanization and Politics in the United States: From Single Model to Multiple Patterns," in *Metropolitanization and Political Change,* eds. Vincenet Hoffman-Martinot and J.M. Sellers (Wiesbaden: Verlag für Sozialwissenschaften, 2005), 53–78.

9. Peter Drier, John Mollenkopf, and Todd Swanstrom, *Place Matters: Metropolitics for the 21st Century* (Wichita: University Press of Kansas, 2014); Kenneth T. Jackson, *Crabgrass Frontier: The Suburbanization of the United States* (New York: Oxford University Press, 1985).

10. Richard Briffault, "The Local Government Boundary Problem in Metropolitan America," *Stanford Law Review* 48, no. 5 (1996): 1115–1171.

11. Bischoff, "School District Fragmentation"; Erica Frankenberg, "Splintering School Districts: Understanding the Link Between Segregation and Fragmentation," *Law and Social Inquiry* 34, no. 4 (2009): 869–909; Jennifer Jellison Holme and Kara Finnigan, "School Diversity, School District Fragmentation and Metropolitan Policy," *Teachers College Record* 115, no. 11 (2013); Orfield, "Politics and Regionalism"; Myron Orfield and Thomas Luce, *Region: Planning the Future of The Twin Cities* (Minneapolis: University of Minnesota Press, 2010).

12. Paul A. Jargowsky, "Sprawl, Concentration of Poverty, and Urban Inequality," in *Urban Sprawl: Causes, Consequences and Policy Responses,* ed. Gregory Spires (Washington, DC: Urban Institute Press, 2001); john a. powell, "Addressing Regional Dilemmas for Minority Communities," in *Reflections On Regionalism*, ed. Bruce Katz (Washington, DC: Brookings Institution Press, 2000), 218–248.

13. Jargowsky, "Sprawl"; G. D. Squires and C. E. Kubrin, "Privileged Places: Race, Uneven Development, and the Geography of Opportunity in Urban America," *Urban Studies* 42, no. 1 (2005): 47–68.

14. Jargowsky, "Sprawl."

15. Jargowsky, "Sprawl."

16. See, for example, Richard Briffault, "The Local Government Boundary Problem in Metropolitan America," *Stanford Law Review* 48, no. 5 (1996): 1115–1171; Gerald E. Frug, "Beyond Regional Government," *Harvard Law Review* 115, no. 7 (2002): 1763–1836; Orfield, "Politics and Regionalism."

17. powell, "Addressing Regional Dilemmas," 236.
18. See also, Drier et al., *Place Matters,* 242.
19. Orfield, "Politics and Regionalism," 143.
20. "This Is The Supervisors Inter-County Committee: How Six Michigan Counties Are Solving Common Problems," https://babel.hathitrust.org/cgi/pt?id=mdp.39015071192440;view=1up;seq=1
21. "This Is The Supervisors Inter-County Committee," 4.
22. *Milliken v. Bradley,* 345 F. Supp. 914 (E.D. Mich. 1972).
23. *Milliken v. Bradley,* at 804–805.
24. Richard Briffault, "The Local Government Boundary Problem in Metropolitan America," *Stanford Law Review* 48, no. 5 (1996): 1115–1171; Vogel and Harrigan, *Political Change*; Orfield, "Politics and Regionalism."
25. Vogel and Harrigan, *Political Change*, 308.
26. Orfield, "Politics and Regionalism," 144.
27. Vogel and Harrigan, *Political Change*, 308.
28. Orfield, "Politics and Regionalism," 137.
29. Alan Altshuler, William Morrill, Harold Wolman, and Faith Mitchell, eds., *Governance and Opportunity in Metropolitan America* (Washington, DC: Committee on Improving the Future of US Cities Through Improved Metropolitan Governance, National Research Council, 1999).
30. Altshuler et al., *Governance and Opportunity*; Vogel and Harrigan, *Political Change*.
31. Robert E. England, John P. Pelissero, and David R. Morgan, *Managing Urban America* (Thousand Oaks, CA: CQ Press, 2017), 62.
32. Drier et al., *Place Matters*; Myron Orfield and Thomas Luce, *Region: Planning the Future of the Twin Cities* (Minneapolis, MN: University of Minnesota Press, 2010).
33. *Minnesota State Statutes*, section 473.145, https://www.revisor.mn.gov/statutes/?id=473.145.
34. Metro Council, *History of the Council*, https://metrocouncil.org/About-Us/What-We-Do/History-of-the-Metropolitan-Council.aspx.
35. Vogel and Harrigan, *Political Change,* 312.
36. powell, "Addressing Regional Dilemmas."
37. Orfield, "Politics and Regionalism."
38. Derek Thompson, "The Miracle Of Minneapolis," *The Atlantic*, March 2015.
39. Orfield, "Politics and Regionalism," 107.
40. Thompson, "The Miracle of Minneapolis."
41. Orfield, "Politics and Regionalism," 105–106.
42. Orfield, *Metropolitics*
43. Orfield and Luce, *Region: Planning the Future*, 79. Also Myron Orfield and Will Stancil, "Why Are the Twin Cities So Segregated?," *Mitchell Hamline Law Review* 43, no. 1 (2017), 1–58.
44. Orfield and Luce, *Region: Planning the Future*.
45. Orfield and Stancil, "Why Are the Twin Cities."
46. Orfield and Stancil, "Why Are the Twin Cities," 10.
47. Orfield and Stancil, "Why Are the Twin Cities," 10.
48. Orfield and Stancil, "Why Are the Twin Cities," 11.
49. Orfield and Stancil, "Why Are the Twin Cities," 2–3.

50. Orfield and Stancil, "Why Are the Twin Cities," 3.

51. 473.145 Development Guide (Minnesota 2017), https://www.revisor.mn.gov /statutes/?id=473.145; *Minnesota Statutes*, section 473.145 (emphasis added).

52. Alejandra Matos, MaryJo Webster, and Anthony Lonetree, "Urban School Districts Are Among Least Integrated," *StarTribune*, November 2, 2015, http://www.star tribune.com/urban-school-districts-are-among-least-integrated/339132801/.

53. Neil Kraus, "Concentrated Poverty and Urban School Reform: 'The Choice is Yours' in Minneapolis," *Equity and Excellence in Education* 41, no. 2 (2008), 267, http:doi .org/10.1080/10665680801911250.

54. Kara Finnigan et al., "Regional Educational Policy Analysis: Rochester, Omaha, and Minneapolis' Inter-District Arrangements," *Educational Policy* 29, vol 5 (2015): 780–814.

55. Myron Orfield and Baris Gumus-Dawes, "When the Feds Won't Act: School Deseg- regation, State Courts, and Minnesota's 'The Choice Is Yours' Program," *Poverty and Race*, January/February 2008, http://prrac.org/full_text.php?text_id=1164&item _id=11246&newsletter_id=97&header=Education&kc=1.

56. Kim McGuire, "FAIR School Plans Move Ahead Despite Lack of Clarity on Manage- ment," *StarTribune*, May 25, 2015, http://www.startribune.com/fair-school-west -metro-program-move-ahead-with-transitions/304943391/.

57. Drier et al., *Place Matters*, 236.

58. Drier et al., *Place Matters*; Vogel and Harrigan, *Political Change*.

59. Drier et al., *Place Matters,* 261.

60. Arthur C. Nelson, Thomas W. Sanchez, and Casey J. Dawkins, *The Social Impacts of Urban Containment* (New York: Routledge, 2007), 38.

61. Myron Orfield, "Land Use and Housing Policies to Reduce Concentrated Poverty and Racial Segregation," *Fordham Law Journal* 33 (2005): 101–159; Drier et al., *Place Matters,* 262.

62. Vogel and Harrigan, *Political Change;* Drier et al., *Place Matters,* 261.

CHAPTER 5

1. Jennifer Jellison Holme, Sarah L. Diem, and Katherine C. Mansfield, "Regional Coalitions and Educational Policy: Lessons from the Nebraska Learning Commu- nity Agreement," in *Integrating Schools in a Changing Society: New Policies and Legal Options for a Multiracial Generation,* eds. Erica Frankenberg and Elizabeth DeBray (Chapel Hill: University of North Carolina Press, 2011), 151–166; Jennifer Jellison Holme and Sarah Diem, "Regional Governance in Education: A Case Study of the Metro Area Learning Community in Omaha, Nebraska," *Peabody Journal of Educa- tion* 90, no. 1 (2015): 156–177.

2. Holme et al., "Regional Coalitions"; Holme and Diem "Regional Governance."

3. Holme and Diem, "Regional Governance."

4. john a. powell, "Addressing Regional Dilemmas for Minority Communities," in *Reflections On Regionalism,* ed. Bruce Katz (Washington, DC: Brookings Institution Press, 2000), 218–248.

5. powell, "Addressing Regional Dilemmas," 223.

6. David Rusk, *Inside Game/Outside Game: Winning Strategies for Saving Urban America* (Washington, DC: Brookings Institution Press, 2001).

7. powell, "Addressing Regional Dilemmas."

8. As cited in Holme et al., "Regional Coalitions," 10.

9. Joe Dejka, "Learning Community's Shared Levy Gives OPS, Others a Boost; Critics Say System Shouldn't Have 'Winners,'" *Omaha World-Herald*, September 22, 2015, http://www.omaha.com/news/education/learning-community-s-shared-levy-gives -ops-others-a-boost/article_aeaa046c-a7d6-59a3-873c-29966dfcd95b.html.

10. "Learning Community of Douglas and Sarpy Counties: Annual Report" (Omaha, NE, 2011), http://www.learningcommunityds.org/files/1113/5785/9403/2011 _LearningCommunityAnnualReport.pdf.

11. Myron Orfield, *American Metropolitics: The New Suburban Reality* (Washington, DC: The Urban Institute Press, 2002).

12. Holme and Diem, "Regional Governance."

13. "Learning Community of Douglas and Sarpy Counties: Annual Evaluation Report 2013–14," (Omaha, NE, 2015), http://learningcommunityds.org/files/3514/1938 /0655/Learning_Community_2014_Report.pdf.

14. Jennifer Jellison Holme et al., "Studying the Implementation of the Federal Full-Service Community Schools Grant Program" (prepared for presentation at the annual meeting of the American Educational Research Association, April 2017).

15. Terrance L. Green and Mark A. Gooden, "Transforming Out-of-School Challenges into Opportunities: Community Schools Reform in the Urban Midwest," *Urban Education* 49, no. 8 (2014): 931.

16. Anna Maier, Julia Daniel, Jeannie Oakes, and Livia Lam, *Community Schools as an Effective School Improvement Strategy: A Review of the Evidence* (Palo Alto, CA: Learning Policy Institute, 2017).

17. Manuel Pastor, Chris Benner, and Martha Matsouka, *This Could Be the Start of Something Big: How Social Movements for Regional Equity Are Reshaping Metropolitan America* (Ithaca, NY: Cornell University Press, 2009).

18. Rachel G. Bratt and William M. Rohe, "Challenges and Dilemmas Facing Community Development Corporations in the United States," *Community Development Journal* 42, no. 1 (2005): 63–78, https://doi.org/10.1093/cdj/bsi092.

19. Pastor et al., *This Could Be the Start*, 8.

20. "Overview: Community Development Corporations (CDCs)," Community-Wealth .org, https://community-wealth.org/strategies/panel/cdcs/index.html.

21. George Galster et al., *The Impact of Community Development Corporations on Urban Neighborhoods* (Washington, DC: The Urban Institute, 2005), 3.

22. Rusk, *Inside Game/Outside Game,* 18.

23. Rusk, *Inside Game/Outside Game,* 18.

24. Pastor et al., *This Could Be the Start*, 9.

25. Joe Dejka, "Learning Community Property Tax Hike Is Cost of 'About a Soda' to Average Homeowner, Finance Director Says," *Omaha World-Herald*, August 25, 2017, http://www.omaha.com/news/education/learning-community-property-tax-hike-is -cost-of-about-a/article_87b8c799-40a2-5c3d-b3eb-1869573df823.html.

26. powell, "Addressing Regional Dilemmas," 239.

27. As cited in Holme et al., "Regional Coalitions."

28. "Learning Community of Douglas and Sarpy Counties: Annual Evaluation Report 2015–16," (Omaha, NE, 2016). http://www.learningcommunityds.org/news/reports/.

29. Nebraska Department of Education, *Enrollment Option Program; Frequently Asked Questions*. (Lincoln, NE, 2017), http://www.education.ne.gov/FOS/OrgServices /EnrollmentOption/.

30. Amanda E. Lewis and John B. Diamond, *Despite the Best Intentions: How Racial Inequality Thrives in Good Schools* (New York: Oxford University Press, 2017); See also Amy Stuart Wells, Jennifer Jellison Holme, Anita Tijerina Revilla, and Awo Korantemaa Atanda, *Both Sides Now: The Story of Desegregation's Graduates* (Berkeley: University of California Press, 2009).

31. Research has found that providing vouchers in high opportunity neighborhoods yields significant gains in long-term outcomes, and for those children who attended low poverty schools, also short-term educational gains. See Raj Chetty, Nathaniel Hendren, and Lawrence Katz, *The Effects of Exposure to Better Neighborhoods on Children: New Evidence from the Moving to Opportunity Experiment* (Cambridge, MA: Harvard University and National Bureau of Economic Research, 2015). See also Marjorie A. Turner, Austin Nichols, and Jennifer Comey, *Benefits Of Living in High-Opportunity Neighborhoods: Insights from the Moving to Opportunity Demonstration* (Washington, DC: The Urban Institute, 2012).

32. Myron Orfield and Thomas Luce, *Region: Planning the Future of the Twin Cities* (Minneapolis: University of Minnesota Press, 2010), 127; see also Stacy E. Seicsh-naydre, "How Government Housing Perpetuates Racial Segregation: Lessons from Post-Katrina New Orleans," *Catholic University Law Review* 60, no. 3 (2011), http:// scholarship.law.edu/lawreview/vol60/iss3/5.

33. Robert Dietz, "How Many People Have Benefitted from the Affordable Housing Credit?," Eye on Housing, http://eyeonhousing.org/2015/11/how-many-people -have-benefitted-from-the-affordable-housing-credit/; see also John Eligon, Yamiche Alcindor, and Agustin Armendariz, "Program to Spur Low Income Housing Is Keeping Cities Segregated," *New York Times*, July 2, 2017, https://www.nytimes .com/2017/07/02/us/federal-housing-assistance-urban-racial-divides.html; and Keren Mertens Horn and Katherine O'Regan, "The Low Income Housing Tax Credit and Racial Segregation," NYU Furman Center, http://furmancenter.org/research /publication/the-low-income-housing-tax-credit-and-racial-segregation.

34. Genevieve Siegel-Hawley, *When the Fences Come Down: Twenty-First Century Lessons from Metropolitan School Desegregation* (Chapel Hill: University of North Carolina Press, 2016).

35. Lynn M. Ross, Rachelle L. Levitt, and Chase Sackett, "Insights: Breaking Down Bar-riers: Housing, Neighborhoods, and Schools of Opportunity," (Washington, DC: US Department of Housing and Urban Development Office of Policy Development and Research), 21. Although use of these scores alone is limiting, this attempt to include schools in the index is noteworthy.

36. Texas Low Income Housing Information Service, *Fair Housing and Balanced Choices: Did Texas Reduce Government-Funded Segregation?* (Austin, TX: Texas Low Income Housing Information Service, 2017).

37. Erica Frankenberg and Gary Orfield, eds., *The Resegregation of Suburban Schools: A Hidden Crisis in American Education* (Cambridge, MA: Harvard Education Press, 2012).

38. Ronald Vogel and John Harrigan, *Political Change in the Metropolis* (New York: Pearson Education, 2007); Peter Drier, John Mollenkopf, and Todd Swanstrom,

Place Matters: Metropolitics for the Twenty-First Century (Wichita: University Press of Kansas, 2014), 261; Myron Orfield, *Metropolitics: A Regional Agenda for Community and Stability* (Washington, D.C: Brookings Institution Press, 1997).

39. Jennifer Jellison Holme, Sarah L. Diem, and Katherine Mansfield, *Using Regional Coalitions to Address Socioeconomic Isolation: The Creation of the Nebraska Learning Community Agreement* (Cambridge, MA: Charles Hamilton Houston Institute for Race and Justice at Harvard Law School, 2009), 14.

40. powell, "Addressing Regional Dilemmas," 234.

41. As cited in Holme et al., "Regional Coalition," 28.

42. Holme and Diem, "Regional Governance."

43. See, for example, Houston: "GO Neighborhood," Neighborhood Recovery Community Development Corporation, http://nrcdc.org/site/programs/go-neighborhood/.

44. One potential example of this is Chicanos Por La Causa, a CDC in Arizona that runs schools. "What Sets Us Apart," Chicanos Por La Causa, https://www.cplc.org/About Us/WhatSetsUsApart/.

45. As cited in Holme et al., "Regional Coalitions," 28.

46. As cited in Holme and Diem, "Regional Governance."

CHAPTER 6

1. Richard Thompson Ford, "The Boundaries of Race: Political Geography in Legal Analysis," *Harvard Law Review* 107, no. 8 (1994): 1845, doi:10.2307/1341760.

2. Peter Dreier, John Mollenkopf, and Todd Swanstrom, *Place Matters: Metropolitics for the Twenty-First Century* (Lawrence: University Press of Kansas, 2004), 246.

3. Marion Orr and Valerie C. Johnson, *Power in the City* (Lawrence: University Press of Kansas, 2008); Clarence N. Stone, Jeffrey R. Henig, Bryan D. Jones, and Carol Pierannunzi, *Building Civic Capacity: The Politics of Reforming Urban Schools* (Lawrence: University Press of Kansas, 2001); Jeffrey R. Henig, Richard C. Hula, Marion Orr, and Desiree S. Pedescleaux, *The Color of School Reform* (Princeton, NJ: Princeton University, 1999).

4. Stone et al., *Building Civic Capacity*.

5. Todd Swanstrom, Will Winter, Margaret Sherraden, and Jessica Lake, "Civic Capacity and School/Community Partnerships in a Fragmented Suburban Setting: The Case of 24:1," *Journal of Urban Affairs* 35, no. 1 (2013): 25, doi:10.1111/juaf.12005.

6. Manuel Pastor, Chris Benner, and Martha Matsuoka, *This Could Be the Start of Something Big: How Social Movements for Regional Equity Are Reshaping Metropolitan America* (Ithaca, NY: Cornell University Press, 2009); Margaret Weir, "Coalition Building for Regionalism," in *Reflections on Regionalism,* ed. Bruce Katz (Washington DC: Brookings Institution Press, 2000), 127–153.

7. Dorothy Shipps, "Pulling Together: Civic Capacity and Urban School Reform," *American Educational Research Journal* 40, no. 4 (2003): 841–878, doi:10.3102 /00028312040004841.

8. As cited in Jennifer Jellison Holme, Sarah L. Diem and Katherine Cumings Mansfield, "Regional Coalitions and Educational Policy: Lessons from the Nebraska Learning Community" in *Integrating Schools in a Changing Society: New Policies and Legal Options for a Multiracial Generation,* eds. Erica Frankenberg and Elizabeth Debray (Chapel Hill: University of North Carolina Press, 2011).

9. Weir, "Coalition Building for Regionalism."

10. Manuel Pastor, Chris Benner, and Martha Matsuoka, "For What It's Worth: Regional Equity, Community Organizing, and Metropolitan America," *Journal of the Community Development Society* 42, no. 4 (2011): 442, doi:10.1080/15575330.2010.532877.

11. Angela Blackwell and Radhika K. Fox, *Regional Equity and Smart Growth: Opportunities for Advancing Social and Economic Justice in America* (Coral Gables, FL: Funders' Network for Smart Growth and Livable Communities, 2004).

12. John W. Kingdon, *Agendas, Alternatives, and Public Policies* (Boston: Little Brown, 2003).

13. John W. Kingdon, *Agendas, Alternatives, and Public Policies* (Boston: Little Brown, 1984): 129.

14. Michael Mintrom and Phillipa Norman, "Policy Entrepreneurship and Policy Change," *The Policy Studies Journal* 37, no. 4 (2009): 650.

15. Michael Mintrom, "Policy Entrepreneurs and the Diffusion of Innovation," *American Journal of Political Science* 41, no. 4 (1997): 738–70.

16. Stone et al., *Building Civic Capacity*; Swanstrom et al., "Civic Capacity and School/Community Partnerships," 25.

17. Robert J. Chaskin, Prudence Brown, Sudhir Venkatesh, and Avid Vidal, *Building Community Capacity* (New York: Aldine, 2001); Dana L. Mitra, William C. Frick, and Marcela A. Movit, "Brain Drain in the Rust Belt: Can Educational Reform Help to Build Civic Capacity in Struggling Communities?" *Educational Policy* 22 (2008): 731–757, doi:10.1177/0895904807310038; John Portz, Lana Stein, and Robin R. Jones, *City Schools and City Politics* (Lawrence: University Press of Kansas, 1999).

18. "Heartland 2050," http://heartland2050.org/vision/vision/.

19. Pastor et al., "For What It's Worth," 437–457, doi:10.1080/15575330.2010.532877. Derrick A. Bell Jr., "*Brown v. Board of Education* and the Interest-Convergence Dilemma,"

20. *Harvard Law Review* 93, no. 3 (1980): 518–34.

21. Justin Driver, "Rethinking the Interest-Convergence Thesis," *Northwestern University Law Review* 105, no. 1 (2011): 149–197, https://scholarlycommons.law.northwestern.edu/cgi/viewcontent.cgi?&httpsredir=1&article=1182&context=nulr.

22. Richard H. Milner IV, "Critical Race Theory and Interest Convergence as Analytic Tools in Teacher Education Policies and Practices," *Journal of Teacher Education* 59 no. 4 (2008): 332–346, doi:10.1177/0022487108321884.

23. Jennifer Jellison Holme, Sarah Diem, and Katherine Cumings Mansfield, *Using Regional Coalitions to Reduce Socioeconomic Isolation: The Creation of the Nebraska Learning Community Agreement* (Cambridge, MA: Charles Hamilton Houston Institute for Race & Justice, 2009).

24. Myron Orfield, *American Metropolitics: The New Suburban Reality* (Washington, DC: The Urban Institute Press, 2002).

25. Richard Milner, "Critical Race Theory and Interest Convergence."

26. Pastor et al., "For What It's Worth," 452, doi:10.1080/15575330.2010.532877.

27. john a. powell, "Addressing Regional Dilemmas for Minority Communities" in *Reflections on Regionalism*, ed. Bruce Katz (Washington DC: Brookings Institution Press, 2000).

28. powell, "Addressing Regional Dilemmas."

29. powell, "Addressing Regional Dilemmas," 242, (emphasis added).

30. John Kuscera and Gary Orfield, *New York's Extreme School Segregation: Inequality, Inaction, and a Damaged Future* (Los Angeles: The Civil Rights Project, 2014).

31. New York State Regional Economic Development Councils, https://regionalcouncils .ny.gov.

32. New York State Regional Economic Development Council Initiatives, https://www .labor.ny.gov/workforce/swib/docs/2013redcworkforcedevelopmentgoals.pdf.

33. Christopher A. Suarez, "Reducing Isolation through School Innovation Grants," *Education Law & Policy Review* 3 (2016): 90–140.

34. Maryland Commission on Innovation and Excellence in Education, *Preliminary Report*, (2018), 77, http://dls.maryland.gov/pubs/prod/NoPblTabMtg/CmsnIn novEduc/2018-Preliminary-Report-of-the-Commission.pdf.

35. United States Department of Housing and Urban Development, United States Department of Education, & United States Department of Transportation, *Dear Colleagues Letter*, June 3, 2016, https://www2.ed.gov/documents/press-releases /06032016-dear-colleagues-letter.pdf.

ACKNOWLEDGMENTS

WE WANT TO THANK both the people and organizations who generously lent their time and support to our work. We are extremely grateful to the Ford Foundation for supporting the research that is central to this book. The Ford Foundation project was a collaborative effort with Myron Orfield, Thomas Luce, Sarah Diem, and Allison Mattheis, and both the original fieldwork and our research discussions over the years inspired this book. We also want to thank Phil Tegeler, Susan Eaton, Gina Chirichingo, the Poverty and Race Research Action Council, and the National Coalition on School Diversity, who worked with us on convening meetings of the interdistrict integration programs, who facilitated sharing our research with broader audiences, and who have been leaders in this area.

Our work has also benefitted from the support and encouragement of many colleagues over the years. Special thanks to Jeannie Oakes for her inspiration and support of us and our work. We would also like to thank Sonya Douglass Horsford, Mark Gooden, Bill Tate, and Erica Frankenberg for their important feedback on pieces of this work. We are especially grateful to Janelle Scott, Tina Trujillo, and Elizabeth DeBray not only for their wonderful scholarship that has strengthened our thinking around policy and equity, but also because we know we can always count on them for engaging conversation and a well-deserved night out whenever we are in the same place at once. Jennifer is grateful for the support of Amy Stuart Wells, Gary Orfield, Susan Eaton, Cynthia Osborne, Jennifer Ralls, Camille Wilson, Susan Auerbach, and Lucila Ek. Kara thanks Alan Daly, Julie Marsh, Kyo Yamashiro, Bill Penuel, Betheny Gross, and sean reardon for their friendship and support over the years.

We also want to thank our students, both at the University of Texas and the University of Rochester, who challenged and deepened our thinking through sharing their own stories, perspectives, and experiences. Special thanks also to the students who provided research assistance on this project, including former UT Austin students Joanna Sanchez, who created the GIS maps; Stephen Spring; and Katherine Mansfield; and current and former students at the University of Rochester including Tricia Stewart, Burke Scarbrough, Nadine Hylton, Tom Noel, Jenny Lafleur, and Atiya Smith. And thanks to Christina Curti and Michelle Kennedy who jumped in during the final crunch.

We owe a great deal of gratitude to Caroline Chauncey at Harvard Education Press for her encouragement of our initial elevator speech, and for her patience, support, and incredibly thoughtful insights along the way. Her enthusiasm helped us move forward at various times when we got stuck, and her sharp eye made our work so much better. We also want to thank Jeff Henig for early conversations and feedback that were extremely valuable as we embarked on this project and pushed our thinking in important ways around the political dynamics at play.

Jennifer wants to thank her family, especially Troy, Katie, and Anna for their humor, love, and support throughout this project, and Robert Jellison and Nancy O'Connor for inspiring her commitment to equity and social justice. Kara wants to thank Anne, Cullen, Steve, and Danielle for countless discussions about these and related issues, and Maya, Hugh, and Kelly for their love, laughter, and ongoing conversations about racial justice and equity.

ABOUT THE AUTHORS

JENNIFER JELLISON HOLME is associate professor of education policy in the College of Education at the University of Texas at Austin. Her research agenda focuses on the politics and implementation of educational policy, with a focus on the relationship between school reform, equity, and diversity in schools. Her work is particularly centered on the ways in which patterns of racial and ethnic stratification interact with educational policies to shape opportunities, experiences, and outcomes for students. She has researched and published on school desegregation, school choice, high-stakes testing, and teacher turnover. Holme earned her PhD in Education Policy from UCLA, her EdM in Administration, Planning, and Social Policy from the Harvard Graduate School of Education, and her BA in Sociology from UCLA.

KARA S. FINNIGAN, a professor at the University of Rochester's Warner School of Education, focuses on educational policy implementation, racial equity, and urban education. Finnigan has written extensively on the topics of low-performing schools and high-stakes accountability, district reform, desegregation, and school choice. Her research blends perspectives in education, sociology, and political science and employs both qualitative and quantitative methods, including social-network analysis and GIS mapping. Beyond her research on interdistrict integration policies and regional equity that is the focus of this book, her recent work examines the role of social networks in the diffusion of research evidence at the school and district levels, as well as community engagement and advocacy around educational change. Finnigan began her work in education as a substitute teacher in Anchorage, Alaska. She received her PhD in Education Policy from the University of Wisconsin-Madison, her MA in Administration and Policy Analysis from Stanford University, and a BA from Dartmouth College.

INDEX